GRE® **Math Simplified with Video Solutions**

Video Access

To view the videos that accompany this book, visit:

http://www.andrewstutoring.com or our YouTube Channel: Andrews Tutoring.

But don't forget to try the practice sets first!

If you have any concerns, please contact Andrews Tutoring at julia@andrewstutoring.com.

ISBN 9781481116619
COPYRIGHT 2013

Credits and Acknowledgements

A heartfelt thanks to the people who have contributed to this project:

Illustrator: Ron Leishman (toonclipart.com)

Editors: Lara Andrews, Ian MacIntire, and Rosalind Taylor

Videographers: Parrish Stinson and Rosalind Taylor

Consultant: Mary Ann Green Stinson

Table of Contents

Page

1) Letter to Soon-to-Be Grad Student   9

2) On Your Mark, Get Set... (General Study Tips)   11

3) Study Road Map   13

4) About the GRE   15

5) Chapter 1: Your Number's Up (Number Properties)   19

6) Chapter 2: Not Quite Whole
    (Fractions, Decimals, and Percents)   50

7) Chapter 3: Things Will Balance Out
    (Ratios and Proportions)   75

8) Chapter 4: Run Of the Mill
    (Averages and Other Statistical Measures)   99

9) Chapter 5: Express Yourself! (Expressions)   115

10) Chapter 6: Balance Beam (Equations and Inequalities)   128

11) Chapter 7: I Thought This Was MATH, Not English!
    (Word Problems)   152

12) Chapter 8: Let Me Get This Straight
    (Lines and Angles)   175

13) Chapter 9: Shape Up! (Triangles and Other Polygons)   186

14) Chapter 10: You Have Me Running in ... (Circles)   207

15) Chapter 11: 3-D (Solid Figures)   219

16) Chapter 12: Gettin' Down to The Nitty Grid-dy
    (Coordinate Geometry)   228

17) Chapter 13: What're the Odds?
    (Counting and Probability)   246

18) Chapter 14: Map it Out (Data Interpretation)   266

19) Chapter 15: Strategies 101   285

20) About the Author   297

Dear Soon-to-Be Grad Student:

Welcome to **GRE Math Simplified with Video Solutions**!

I wrote this book to reach prospective graduate students like you and the ones I've been tutoring over the last 10 years— bright students and professionals who are looking for rigorous, affordable GRE preparation. The majority of my students have either forgotten math concepts or are in need of learning them for the first time. Some are short on time, money, or both. Almost all need a review of the basics, familiarity with "GRE speak," and lessons delivered in a way that resonate with them. If this sounds familiar, this book is for you.

Over the last decade, I've successfully explained standardized math concepts— including GRE math— to hundreds of students, learning what barriers have prevented them from understanding certain concepts and what it takes for them to "get it." I've incorporated this knowledge and these experiences into this book, explaining math basics, identifying how concepts are tested and how to determine what is being asked, and explaining nuances across problems.

In addition, some of my students have asked to record our sessions so that they could re-play them when they got stuck, giving me the idea to record the video solutions. I know it can be hard to learn math from a textbook alone, and sometimes an oral explanation makes all the difference.

GRE Math Simplified problems are of three types: check-ins, examples, and problems for practice sets. Check-ins are problems that provide practice of the fundamental or prerequisite skill. Examples are GRE-style questions embedded within the chapter and require application of the concept most recently explained. Practice set problems are also GRE-style questions. Located at the end of each chapter, practice sets rely on a mix of the concepts presented in the chapter and correspond to a solutions video.

GRE Math Simplified will help you: 1) eliminate holes in your math foundation, 2) learn GRE math concepts in a straightforward, comprehensive way, and 3) build confidence and know how for the exam. It is intended to be used with the video solutions, and is indexed to **The Official Guide to the Revised General Test (2nd Edition)** for extra practice.

Good luck!

Julia Andrews
Founder, Andrews Tutoring

On Your Mark, Get Set...!
(Getting Started)

Your first math lesson is to figure out how to pace yourself through this material. Whether you have two weeks, two months, or more (or, gulp, less) to prepare, we can keep you busy! There are 15 math-focused chapters in this manual. Based on your timeline, decide how much time you can dedicate to mastering the concepts in each chapter. Note that your goal should be to master each concept, not simply "read and move on." That means you might need to read a chapter multiple times or re-play a video. Digesting the material in this book is key to success.

Tips to Boost Your Score:

1) Familiarize yourself with all the problem types before you take the test. Some questions require you to come up with your own answer. Other questions require you to compare quantities. Still others have more than one answer. Learn to distinguish between the different problem types. This will ensure that you don't misunderstand the directions or lose time trying to process them on test day.

2) Follow the Suggested Study Plan if you are planning a comprehensive review program. This includes purchasing **The Official Guide to the GRE Revised General Test (2nd Edition).**

3) Read each chapter and complete the practice exercises to the best of your ability. Check your answers and, for the ones you got wrong, try to identify why the correct answer is right and where your approach might have been wrong. For any section in which you struggle, watch the accompanying video solutions for that chapter. Listen to the explanations and then go back and re-try the problems.

4) After each chapter, complete the suggested problems (as indicated in the Study Plan) in **The Official Guide (2nd Edition).**

5) Every few chapters, go back and review what you learned.
Remember: "Review it or lose it!"

6) Take ALL four of the practice tests from The Official Guide (2nd Edition), particularly the two computer-based practice tests. Taking practice tests written by the test writers will help you develop a proper sense of pacing, reduce test anxiety, and build stamina so you can remain calm and alert throughout your test.

7) Study regularly. On the whole, you will process more information if you study for one or two hours a day, five days a week, than you will if you concentrate large blocks of study time to, say, the weekend. It also helps to study around the time of day that you intend to take the test. While this might not always be possible, take advantage when it is.

8) Time yourself. But time yourself wisely. Don't time yourself when you first learn a concept or when you are first working through the practice set at the end of each chapter. This will likely only frustrate you. It takes longer to work through problems when you first encounter a topic. So, take your time to work through the problems in this book— but when you move on to the **Official Guide** problems, time yourself— **allowing approximately one minute and 45 seconds per problem.**

Suggested Study Plan for GRE Math Simplified

Assignment	GRE Math Simplified	GRE Math Simplified Video	ETS' Revised GRE (2nd Edition)
Practice Test 1- CD ROM (Diagnostic)			CD-Rom (Official Guide)
Familiarize yourself with the GRE	Read pages 15-17		Read pages: 1-10 (General), 11-42 (Essay), 43-52 (Verbal), 107-109 & 129-130 (Math)
Number Properties	Chapter 1	Chapter 1 Solutions	p. 110- #1 p. 114- #7 p. 118- #2 p. 121- #1-2 p. 123- #4 p. 219- #1, 3-8, 14, & 15 p. 244- #5
Fractions, Decimals, and Percents	Chapter 2	Chapter 2 Solutions	p. 111- #3 p.126- #4 p. 219-220- #2, 9-12 p. 244- #11
Ratios	Chapter 3	Chapter 3 Solutions	p. 220- #13 p. 244- #10
Averages	Chapter 4	Chapter 4 Solutions	p. 122- #3 p. 296-298 #1-3, 16
Expressions	Chapter 5	Chapter 5 Solutions	p. 113- #6 p. 115- #8-9 p. 243- #1-2
Equations and Inequalities	Chapter 6	Chapter 6 Solutions	p. 112- #5 p. 117- #1 p. 244- #6-8
Word Problems	Chapter 7	Chapter 7 Solutions	p. 110- #2 p. 119- #4 p. 124- #1 p. 244- #9, 12-16
Lines and Angles	Chapter 8	Chapter 8 Solutions	p. 259- #1

Assignment	GRE Math Simplified	GRE Math Simplified Video	ETS' Revised GRE (2nd Edition)
Triangles and Other Polygons	Chapter 9	Chapter 9 Solutions	p. 111- #4 p. 125- #2 p. 259- #2-11
Circles	Chapter 10	Chapter 10 Solutions	p. 245- 20 p. 261- #12-13
Solid Figures	Chapter 11	Chapter 11 Solutions	p. 262- #14
Coordinate Geometry	Chapter 12	Chapter 12 Solutions	p. 118- #3 p. 243-#3-4 p. 245- #17-19
Probability and Statistics	Chapter 13	Chapter 13 Solutions	p.120 -#5 p. 297- #6-15
Data Analysis	Chapter 14	Chapter 14 Solutions	p. 125- #3 p. 127 - #1-3 p. 296-299- #5, 17-19
Strategies	Chapter 15		
Practice Set- Easy			p. 145-149 (all) p. 164 (Answers)
Practice Set- Medium			p. 150-154 (all) p. 164 (Answers)
Practice Set- Hard			p.155-160 (all) p. 165 (Answers)
Practice Set- Data Interpretation			p. 161-163- all p. 165 (Answers)
Practice Test 1- Book			p. 303-430
Practice Test 2- Book			p. 431-563
Practice Test 2- CD Rom			CD-Rom (Official Guide)

About the GRE

The Educational Testing Service (ets.org), the maker of the GRE, is the best place to learn about all things GRE, from scoring to test locations to how to sign up for the exam. I encourage you to spend some time on the ETS website or in the introductory chapters of the Official Guide to learn as much as you can. Following are some of the most important things you need to know about the GRE.

Structure:

The first section of the GRE is the analytical writing portion of the test, in which you are required to write two essays. Following this section are two sections each of verbal reasoning and quantitative reasoning, which can appear in any order. There are 20 questions per verbal and quantitative section.

The computer selects your second section of each verbal and quantitative section based on how well you do on the first section of that type. You might also get an experimental section in either verbal or quantitative reasoning on your test. The experimental section will be indistinguishable from the other sections, so you will have to try just as hard in that section even though it won't count towards your score.

Math Question Types:

There are **four types of math questions** on the Revised GRE.

1) **Multiple Choice with One Correct Answer:** This is your standard multiple choice format, where you are directed to choose the correct answer.

2) **Multiple Choice with One or More Correct Answers:** This multiple choice format requires you to select all correct answers. There will be one or more correct answers. To receive credit, you must select all of the correct answer choices.

3) **Quantitative Comparison:** This question format presents the problem in the form of two columns, Quantity A and Quantity B. You are to compare the two columns and select answer:

a) if the value in Quantity A is always greater,
b) if the value in Quantity B is always greater,
c) if Quantity A and Quantity B are always equal, or
d) if the relationship between the columns cannot be determined.

4) **Numeric Entry:** This question format requires you to calculate your own answer and enter it into a solution box.

Scoring and Percentiles:

The Revised GRE is based on a scoring scale that ranges from 130 to 170 in 1-point increments for both the verbal and quantitative reasoning sections. These scores are based on your raw score, which is the number of questions you answer correctly. The analytical writing section is scored from 0 to 6 in half-point increments.

Percent of Test Takers Who Scored Lower Than Selected Scaled Scores

Scaled Score	Quantitative	Verbal Reasoning
170	99	99
165	95	92
160	83	81
155	65	64
150	44	43
145	24	23
140	10	9
135	3	2

*Data from ETS. Table 1A: Verbal Reasoning and Quantitative Reasoning Interpretative Data on Score Reports (Based on the performance of all examinees who tested between 8/1/11 and 4/30/12). ets.org.

Timing:

You have 30 minutes to write each of your two essays. You have 30 minutes per verbal section and 35 minutes per quantitative section.

Changes in Test Experience:

There are some neat changes in the Revised GRE that will likely reduce your anxiety on test day: The new GRE allows you to skip questions and come back to them during the time allotted for that section. Woo hoo! And... (drum roll, please...): The test comes with an **onscreen calculator**! (Don't do the happy dance yet. There is still a lot to learn.)

Seriously, though. Check out ETS's website or the introductory material in the Official Guide. There's good stuff there— and they aren't paying me to say that. In fact, I have no affiliation.

Scheduling Dates:

Schedule your test at ets.org. Keep in mind that you can only take the GRE once every 30 days. In addition, it takes 10-15 days for graduate programs to receive your score. Plan accordingly!

Chapter 1: Your Number's Up
(Number Properties)

You might be thinking, "Why is
there a section on
NUMBERS?" (Fair question.)

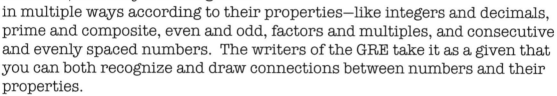

"I know what numbers are. What
clown wrote this?!" (Ok, now you're
taking it too far.)

Well, there are different types of
numbers, and they are categorized
in multiple ways according to their properties—like integers and decimals,
prime and composite, even and odd, factors and multiples, and consecutive
and evenly spaced numbers. The writers of the GRE take it as a given that
you can both recognize and draw connections between numbers and their
properties.

1.1 Integers and Non-Integers

Consider the following number line:

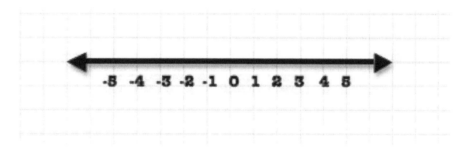

All the numbers written on the number line above are integers. **Integers**
are the counting numbers (1, 2, 3, ...), their opposites (-1, -2, -3,...), and
zero (0).

There are infinitely many non-integers between each of your integers.
For example, between the integers one (1) and two (2) are an infinite
number of numbers, including: 1.278, $\sqrt{2}$, 3/2, and 1.9. So, when the GRE
asks an abstract question that requires you to think of "a number," if it
doesn't specify that it's an integer, or state which type of integer it is,
remember to consider different types of numbers, including: negative,
positive, decimals, fractions, primes, and composites, because different
types of numbers can yield different types of results.

Example 1.1

A number, when squared, becomes: a) bigger, b) smaller, c) the same, d) cannot be determined.

Solution:

d

Depending on what type of number you are squaring, the result can be bigger, smaller, or the same. Therefore, we cannot determine the result without additional information. For example, squaring 5 yields a larger number (25), squaring .60 yields a smaller number (.36), and squaring 1 yields the same number (1).

1.2 Order of Operations

Has this stuck with you since grade school, "**P**lease **E**xcuse **M**y **D**ear **A**unt **S**ally?"

The first letters of each word spell **PEMDAS**, which is a handy mnemonic device for remembering your order of operations. You need to know it to accurately simplify mathematical expressions like:

$$(3-7)^2 + 2 \cdot 8 - 6$$

(And no, you can't just rely on your calculator to get the correct value. Nice try! If you don't input the numbers into the calculator in the proper order, you will not get an accurate result.)

PEMDAS stands for:

P- parentheses (meaning, simplify everything in parentheses)
E- exponents
M-multiplication/**D**-division
A-addition/**S**-subtraction

Quick! Tell me how many steps are in the order of operations!

Six, right? Wrong! Multiplication and division actually merge into one step, as do addition and subtraction. So there are actually only 4 steps.

20

That means, as you simplify an expression, when you reach the multiplication and division step, do whichever comes first in the problem—multiplication or division—reading from left to right. The same holds for addition and subtraction.

Check-in:

Evaluate the following expressions. (That means, "What's the answer?"):

1) $5 - 2^2 + 7$ 2) $(3-9) + 3^4 - 8 + 2$ 3) $4 - (11-4) + 6$

Solutions:

1) 8	2) 69	3) 3
$5 - 2^2 + 7$	$(3-9) + 3^4 - 8 + 2$	$4 - (11-4) + 6$
$5 - 4 + 7$	$-6 + 3^4 - 8 + 2$	$4 - (7) + 6$
$1 + 7$	$-6 + 81 - 8 + 2$	$-3 + 6$
8	69	3

1.3 Distributive Property

The **Distributive Property** can also be used to simplify expressions. It is a method of multiplying a number by a sum or difference of numbers.

Distributive Property: $a(b + c) = a \bullet b + a \bullet c$. The value "a" is being "distributed" to each term in parentheses.

For example, the expression $3(x + 2)$ can be simplified to:

$3(x+2) = 3 \bullet x + 3 \bullet 2 = 3x + 6$

Check-in:

Simplify the following expressions:

1) $5(2 + 6)$ 2) $8(x+4)$ 3) $-3(x-7)$

4) $4-(x-9)$ 5) $4x-5(2-x)$ 6) $2x-9[3-(7+x-3)]$

Solutions:

1) **40**

This problem does not have any unknowns, so you can simply add 2 + 6 to get 8, and multiply the result by 5 to get 40.

To simplify this expression using the distributive property, write :

$5 \bullet 2 + 5 \bullet 6$

$10 + 30$

40

2) **8x + 32**

   $8(x + 4)$

   $8 \bullet x + 8 \bullet 4$

   $8x \quad + 32$

3) **-3x + 21**

   $-3(x - 7)$

   $-3x - 3(-7)$

   $-3x - (-21)$

   $-3x + 21$ Subtracting a negative number is equivalent to adding a positive number.

4) **13 - x**

   $4 - (x - 9)$

   $4 - (x - 9)$ Distribute the minus sign to the (x - 9).

   $4 - x - (-9)$

   $4 - x + 9$ Subtracting a negative number is equivalent to adding a

   $13 - x$ positive number.

5) **9x - 10**

   $4x - 5(2 - x)$

   $4x - 5 \bullet 2 - (-5x)$

   $4x - 10 + 5x$

   $9x - 10$

6) **11x + 9**

Note that the brackets serve the same purpose as parentheses.

$2x - 9[3 - (7 + x - 3)]$

$2x - 9[3 - (4 + x)]$ Simplify within parentheses.

$2x - 9[3 - 4 - x)]$ Distribute the minus sign to the $(4 + x)$

$2x - 9[-1 - x]$ Simplify

$2x - [-9 - 9x]$ Distribute the 9 within the brackets.

$2x + 9 + 9x$ Distribute the negative sign.

$11x + 9$ Simplify

Example 1.2

Simplify the following expression : $5(x + 7) - 4(x + 2)$

Solution:

x + 27

$5(x + 7) - 4(x + 2)$

$5x + 35 - 4x - 8$

$x + 27$

1.4 Absolute Value

The **absolute value** of a number is its distance from zero. If you look at the number line on p. 19 you'll notice that "2" is two units from zero, and "-2" is also two units from zero. Therefore, the absolute value of each number is 2. More generally, a number and its opposite have the same absolute value, and that value is always **non-negative** (either zero or positive). In other words, although the original number can be negative, its absolute value cannot be!

Check-in:

a) $|3| =$

b) $|-3| =$

c) $|-4| =$

d) $-|-5| =$

e) If $|x| = 7$, then x must equal _____.

Solution:

a) 3

b) 3

c) 4

d) -5

e) 7 or -7

Note that while the **absolute value** cannot be negative, the input (in this case, x) can be negative.

Example 1.3

If $|x-8| = 15$, what is the sum of the values of x that satisfy the equation?

Solution:

16

There are two numbers that have 15 as its absolute value. Those numbers are 15 and -15. That means that x-8=15 or x-8=-15.

$$
\begin{array}{rcl}
x-8 = 15 & \text{or} & x-8 = -15 \\
\underline{+8 \quad +8} & & \underline{+8 \quad +8} \\
x = 23 & & x = -7
\end{array}
$$

The sum of 23 and -7 is 16.

1.5 Even and Odd Integers

Integers can be considered even or odd. **Even integers** are divisible by 2; **odd integers** are not divisible by 2. You can determine whether a number is even or odd by noting whether the last digit of the number is even or odd.

Note that zero is an even integer.

Examples of Even Integers:

a) -62   b) 32   c) 1,111,110   d) 2 • x, if x is an integer

Examples of Odd Integers:

a) -3   b) 51   c) 2,227   d) 2 • x + 1, if x is an integer

The relationships of adding, subtracting and multiplying even and odd integers are as follows:

Sum	Difference	Product
Even + Even = Even	Even - Even = Even	Even • Even= Even
Odd + Odd = Even	Odd - Odd = Even	Even • Odd = Even
Even + Odd = Odd	Even - Odd = Odd	Odd • Odd = Odd

There are no such rules for division, because when you find the quotient of two integers (meaning, the result of dividing two integers), you don't always end up with another integer. For example: 5÷3 = 1.66666...

Note: Don't stress if you can't easily memorize rules like these. Since these rules are absolute—meaning they always hold true—just test a specific even number (say, 4) and a specific odd number (say, 3) when a question on even and odd numbers arises.

Check-in:

1) When possible, identify each of the following as even or odd:

a) An even number cubed plus one

b) The product of an integer x and the number 4

c) Twice the sum of 3 and an integer

d) An integer x multiplied by the product of integers y and z

Solution:

1)

a) **Odd:** An even number raised to any positive integer is even. Raising a number to an integer power greater than 1 is repeated multiplication. In this case, we are taking the cube of an even number, say, the number 2, which is equivalent to 2•2•2=8, which is even. Add one (or any odd number, for that matter) to any even number, and the result is odd.

b) **Even:** The product of any integer (even or odd) times any even number – in this case the number 4– is always even.

c) **Even:** Doubling an integer, whether even or odd, will always result in an even integer.

d) **Can't be determined:** This example is asking for the product of integers x, y, and z. If all three numbers are odd, the product is odd. If at least one number is even, the entire product is even.

1.6 Zero

Much ado about... zero.

Zero is a funny little number. It gets a lot of attention given that it's worth absolutely nothing.

Here are some things to remember about the number zero:

1) It is neither negative NOR positive. In fact, it separates negative numbers from positive ones.

2) Zero is an EVEN integer. (Yes, we know we mentioned it before– it's just that important to know.)

3) You cannot divide a number by zero, like 8/0 or 100/0. (Didn't your teacher ever tell you that the world would explode if you tried?)

4) You can, however, divide zero by any number—the result is zero. (Think, if you split nothing up among a group of 8 people, each person gets nothing: 0/8=0.)

5) Zero times any number(s) is zero: $x \cdot 0 = 0$ and $x \cdot y \cdot z \cdot 0 = 0$.

6) Zero plus a number x is that number x: $x + 0 = x$.

1.7 Consecutive Integers

Consecutive means "in a row."

Examples of consecutive integers:

1) 12, 13, 14, 15

2) x, x+1, and x+2

There are also **consecutive even integers** (even integers in a row) and **consecutive odd integers** (odd integers in a row).

Examples of consecutive even integers:

1) -4, -2, 0, 2, 4, 6

2) x, x+2, x+4 (where x is even)

Examples of consecutive odd integers:

1) -3, -1, 1, 3, 5, 7

2) x, x+2, x+4 (where x is odd)

1.8 Divisibility

Now that you can use a calculator on the GRE, you save a lot of time on computation. However, don't be fooled—you still have to know your divisibility rules. Trust me, you'll save a lot of time if you do.

For a number A to be **divisible** by a number B, number B must divide evenly into number A—meaning that it leaves no remainder. For example, 42 is divisible by 7, because 7 goes into 42 exactly 6 times with no remainder: $42 \div 7 = 6$.

1.9 Factors and Multiples

A **factor** of a number A is a number that divides evenly into number A, while a **multiple** of a number A is the product of any integer and that number A.

Examples of factors:

The factors of 12 are: 1, 2, 3, 4, 6, and 12.

> To help you remember the difference between factors and multiples, remember that there are a finite number of factors and a multitude (an infinite number, actually) of multiples.

Examples of multiples:

Multiples of 12 include: ...-12, 0, 12, 24, 36...

1.10 Prime Numbers

A **prime number** is a positive integer greater than one that is only divisible by the number one and itself. The number 2 is the only even prime number (because all other even numbers are divisible by 2), and it is the smallest prime number.

Note that 1 is NOT a prime number. The first 10 prime numbers are: 2, 3, 5, 7, 11, 13, 17, 19, 23, and 29.

Example 1.4

If the sum of three prime numbers is even, then one of the prime numbers must be the number _____.

Solution:

2

In order for the sum of three numbers to be even, either one or all three of them must be even. (Test this out by choosing a few numbers yourself.) Since the numbers in this example are all prime, and there is only one even prime number, then only one of the numbers is even and that even number must be 2.

Composite numbers are positive integers greater than one that are not prime numbers. That is, a composite number is divisible by more than just one and itself. As shown below, note that every composite number is the product of its prime factors.

Show 'Em What You're Made Of!: Factor Tree

A **factor tree** enables you to break down a composite number into the product of its primes. This allows you to simplify expressions or to find commonality among numbers.

To create a factor tree, start with a composite number and create two "limbs" by writing **any** two factors that multiply together to equal that composite number. Continue this process—adding limbs to each factor that can be broken down— until every factor is a prime number.

This is a simple process, as illustrated in the following example.

Ex.: Find the prime factorization of 140.

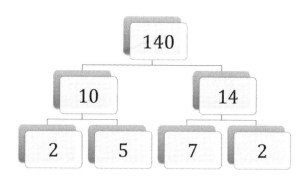

The prime factorization of 140, then, is: $2 \cdot 2 \cdot 5 \cdot 7$, or $2^2 \cdot 5 \cdot 7$.

1.11 Greatest Common Factor (GCF)

The **greatest common factor (GCF)** between two or more numbers is the largest factor that the numbers share— the product of their common prime factors. Identifying the GCF helps simplify expressions and aids in problem solving.

One way to determine the greatest common factor is to make a factor tree for both (or all) of your numbers. Then, circle the prime factors they have in common and multiply one set of these factors together.

For example, find the GCF of 36 and 96:

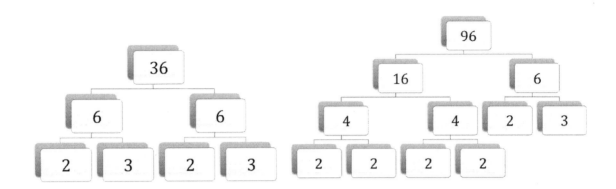

The common prime factors of 36 and 96 are: 2, 2, and 3. Since 2•2•3=12, the GCF is 12.

Check-in:

1) Find the GCF of 18 and 27

2) Find the GCF of 30 and 75

3) Find the GCF of 52 and 91

Solutions:

1) **9**

Prime factorization of 18: $2•3^2$
Prime factorization of 27: 3^3

GCF of 18 and 27 is 3^2=9 (Each number has at least two 3s.)

2) **15**

Prime factorization of 30: $2•3•5$
Prime factorization of 75: $3•5^2$

GCF of 30 and 75 is $3•5$=15 (Each number has one 3 and at least one 5.)

3) **13**

Prime factorization of 52: $2^2 \cdot 13$
Prime factorization of 91: $7 \cdot 13$

GCF of 52 and 91 is 13   (Each number has one 13 and there is no other factor greater than 1 in common.)

1.12 Least Common Multiple (LCM)

The **least common multiple (LCM)** between two or more numbers is the smallest (positive) multiple the numbers have in common. Identifying the LCM can help simplify expressions and aid in problem solving.

One way to find the least common multiple is to break down both (or all) of the numbers into their prime factors, and calculate the product of each prime factor to the highest power of the factor present among the numbers. This is best understood by example:

Find the LCM of 36 and 96:

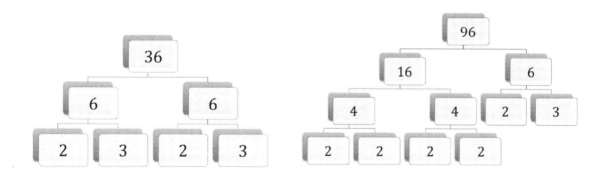

Prime factorization of 36: $2^2 \cdot 3^2$
Prime factorization of 96: $2^5 \cdot 3^1$

To find the LCM you must calculate the product of each prime factor to the highest power of the factor present among the numbers.

Since 36 has factors of 2^2 and 96 has factors of 2^5, include the 2^5 (the higher power of 2) in the least common multiple. Since 36 has factors of 3^2 and 96 a factor of 3^1, include the 3^2 in the least common multiple (the higher power of 3). Thus, the least common multiple is: $2^5 \cdot 3^2 = 288$, the smallest positive number divisible by both 36 and 96.

Check-in:

1) Find the LCM of 18 and 27.

2) Find the LCM of 30 and 75.

3) Find the LCM of 52 and 91.

Solutions:

1) **54**

Prime factorization of 18: $2 \bullet 3^2$
Prime factorization of 27: 3^3

LCM of 18 and 27 is $2 \bullet 3^3 = 54$

2) **150**

Prime factorization of 30: $2 \bullet 3 \bullet 5$
Prime factorization of 75: $3 \bullet 5^2$

LCM of 30 and 75 is $2 \bullet 3 \bullet 5^2 = 150$

3) **364**

Prime factorization of 52: $2^2 \bullet 13$
Prime factorization of 91: $7 \bullet 13$

LCM of 52 and 91 is $2^2 \bullet 7 \bullet 13 = 364$

Example 1.5

What is the product of the greatest common factor and the least common multiple of 12 and 32?

Solution:

384

The GCF is 4 and the LCM is 96, the product of which is 384. [Note that the GCF and LCM of 2 numbers is equal to the product of the original numbers ($32 \bullet 12 = 384$).]

1.13 Exponents and Square Roots

Exponents are used to represent repeated multiplication. For example, to multiply 8 by itself 7 times, instead of writing $8 \bullet 8 \bullet 8 \bullet 8 \bullet 8 \bullet 8 \bullet 8$, simply write 8^7.

Important Rules of Exponents:

1) $(x^y \bullet x^z) = x^{(y+z)}$

(To multiply exponential terms with identical bases, add the exponents.)

Examples:

i. $x^4 \bullet x^7 = x^{11}$

ii. $2y^6 \bullet 6y^3 = 12y^9$

iii. $x^2 y^6 \bullet xy^2 = x^3 y^8$

As in iii, note that if there is no visible power of the variable, it is being raised to a power of 1. For example, in the term xy^2, the variable x is being raised to the first power.

2) $(x^y)^z = x^{(y \bullet z)}$ and $(x \bullet y \bullet z)^b = x^b \bullet y^b \bullet z^b$

(To raise an exponent to another power, multiply the exponents and keep the base.)

Examples:

i. $(x^4)^5 = x^{20}$

ii. $(x^7 y^4 z^2)^3 = x^{21} y^{12} z^6$

iii.) $(3xy)^2 = 3^2 \bullet x^2 \bullet y^2 = 9x^2 y^2$

iv.) $3(xy)^2 = 3 \bullet x^2 \bullet y^2 = 3x^2 y^2$

Note the difference between iii and iv. In iii, the "3" is inside the parentheses and in iv, the "3" is outside the parentheses. In the former, the 3 is raised to the second power and in the latter, the 3 is NOT raised to the second power.

3) x⁰=1

(Any number or variable raised to an exponent of zero is 1.)

Examples:

i. $3^0 = 1$

ii. $(xyz)^0 = x^0 \bullet y^0 \bullet z^0 = 1$

iii. $xyz^0 = x \bullet y \bullet z^0 = x \bullet y \bullet 1 = xy$

Note that, in ii, the zero exponent applies to x, y, and z, because all three variables are in parentheses. In iii, the exponent only applies to z, the variable which is directly in front of it.

4) $ax^y + bx^y = (a+b)x^y$

   $ax^y - bx^y = (a-b)x^y$

[In order to add or subtract terms with the same base and power, add or subtract the **coefficients** (the numbers multiplied to the variables— a and b in this example) and leave the base and exponent unchanged.]

Examples:

i. $3x^4 + 9x^4 = 12x^4$

ii. $-7y^8 - 6y^8 = -13y^8$

iii. $2x^7 + 9x^5$ This expression is already simplified because the two variables are raised to different exponents.

Head's Up: The remaining rules of exponents include working with fractions. If you find that you are having trouble with this section, you may want to review pages 60-65 before preceding.

5) $\dfrac{x^y}{x^z} = x^{(y-z)}$

(When dividing numbers with the same base, subtract the exponents.)

Examples:

i. $\dfrac{x^{12}}{x^{5}} = x^{7}$

ii. $\dfrac{6x^{3}}{2x} = 3x^{2}$

6) $(x)^{-y} = \dfrac{1}{x^{y}}$

(To raise a number to a negative exponent, take the reciprocal of that number and raise it to the absolute value of the exponent).

Examples:

i. $x^{-4} = \dfrac{1}{x^{4}}$

ii. $6x^{-2} = \dfrac{6}{x^{2}}$

iii. $(6x)^{-2} = \dfrac{1}{(6x)^{2}} = \dfrac{1}{36x^{2}}$

7) $\left(\dfrac{x}{y}\right)^{-z} = \left(\dfrac{y}{x}\right)^{z}$

(To raise a fraction to a negative exponent, take the reciprocal of the fraction and raise the result to the absolute value of the exponent.)

Examples:

i. $\left(\dfrac{x^{4}}{y^{5}}\right)^{-3} = \left(\dfrac{y^{5}}{x^{4}}\right)^{3} = \dfrac{y^{15}}{x^{12}}$

ii. $6\left(\dfrac{3x^{2}}{y}\right)^{-2} = 6\left(\dfrac{y}{3x^{2}}\right)^{2} = 6 \bullet \dfrac{y^{2}}{9x^{4}} = \dfrac{6y^{2}}{9x^{4}} = \dfrac{2y^{2}}{3x^{4}}$

Check-in:

Simplify the following expressions using positive exponents:

a) $5x^{2} \bullet 4x^{5}$ b) $3x^{7} \bullet x^{-8}$ c) $(-5x)^{-2}$ d) $5x^{-2}$

e) $\dfrac{40m^7n^2}{5m^3}$ f) $5(x^3)^5$ g) $(5x^3)^5$ h) $\left(\dfrac{x^2}{y^5}\right)^{-1}$

Solution:

a) $20x^7$ b) $\dfrac{3}{x}$ c) $\dfrac{1}{25x^2}$ d) $\dfrac{5}{x^2}$

e) $8m^4n^2$ f) $5x^{15}$ g) $3,125x^{15}$ h) $\dfrac{y^5}{x^2}$

Example 1.6

Given integers m and n, if $m^n\, n^m = 72$, what could be the average of m and n?

Indicate all that apply.

a) -2.5
b) -0.5
c) 0
d) 2.5
e) 5.0

Solution:

d only

In order to find the values of m and n, find the prime factorization of 72, which is $2^3 \bullet 3^2$. Let m=2 and n=3 (or vice versa).

The average, therefore, is $2.5 : \dfrac{2+3}{2}$.

(Note that it does not matter which of the two values is assigned to m or to n, as the question is just asking for the average.)

Example 1.7

If $x^{-5} = \dfrac{1}{32}$, what is x^2?

Solution:

4

$$x^{-5} = \frac{1}{x^5} = \frac{1}{32}$$

$$x^5 = 32$$

Since $2^5 = 32$, $x = 2$. Thus, $x^2 = 4$.

Square Roots

Taking the **square root** of a number is the inverse operation of raising a number to an exponent. A square root can be defined as follows:

> The **square root** of a number a, where a>0, is equal to b if the square of b is equal to a: $\sqrt{a} = b$ if $b^2 = a$.

In other words, the square root of a number x is the number y such that the product of y and y is the number x:

$\sqrt{1} = 1$	$\sqrt{4} = 2$	$\sqrt{9} = 3$	$\sqrt{16} = 4$	$\sqrt{25} = 5$
$\sqrt{36} = 6$	$\sqrt{49} = 7$	$\sqrt{64} = 8$	$\sqrt{81} = 9$	$\sqrt{100} = 10$
$\sqrt{121} = 11$	$\sqrt{144} = 12$	$\sqrt{169} = 13$	$\sqrt{196} = 14$	$\sqrt{225} = 15$
$\sqrt{256} = 16$	$\sqrt{289} = 17$	$\sqrt{324} = 18$	$\sqrt{361} = 19$	$\sqrt{400} = 20$

Note: You cannot take the square root of a negative number under the real number system, because there is no real number, when multiplied by itself, that results in a negative product.

Multiplying Square Roots:

$$\sqrt{a} \cdot \sqrt{b} = \sqrt{ab}$$

Examples:

i. $\sqrt{3} \cdot \sqrt{5} = \sqrt{15}$

ii. $\sqrt{27} = \sqrt{9} \cdot \sqrt{3} = 3\sqrt{3}$

Dividing Square Roots:

$$\frac{\sqrt{a}}{\sqrt{b}} = \sqrt{\frac{a}{b}}$$

Examples:

i. $\dfrac{\sqrt{52}}{\sqrt{13}} = \sqrt{4} = 2$

ii. $\sqrt{\dfrac{x}{36}} = \dfrac{\sqrt{x}}{\sqrt{36}} = \dfrac{\sqrt{x}}{6}$

Check-in:

Simplify the following expressions.

1. $\sqrt{6} \cdot \sqrt{14}$ 2. $\sqrt{5} \cdot \sqrt{5}$ 3. $\sqrt{18} \cdot \sqrt{2}$

4. $\sqrt{\dfrac{42}{3}}$ 5. $\sqrt{\dfrac{98}{2}}$ 6. $\dfrac{\sqrt{22}}{\sqrt{11}}$

Solutions:

1. $\mathbf{2\sqrt{21}}$

$\sqrt{6} \cdot \sqrt{14} = \sqrt{84} = \sqrt{4} \cdot \sqrt{21} = 2 \cdot \sqrt{21} = 2\sqrt{21}$

2. **5**

$\sqrt{5} \cdot \sqrt{5} = \sqrt{25} = 5$ (Note that $\sqrt{x} \cdot \sqrt{x} = x$)

3. **6**

$\sqrt{18} \cdot \sqrt{2} = \sqrt{36} = 6$

4. $\sqrt{\mathbf{14}}$

$\sqrt{\dfrac{42}{3}} = \sqrt{14}$

5. $\sqrt{\mathbf{7}}$

$\sqrt{\dfrac{98}{2}} = \sqrt{49} = 7$

6. $\sqrt{\mathbf{2}}$

$\dfrac{\sqrt{22}}{\sqrt{11}} = \sqrt{\dfrac{22}{11}} = \sqrt{2}$

Simplifying Square Roots

Sometimes you will need to find the square root of a number that is not a perfect square. For example, the $\sqrt{18}$. If you don't need an exact answer, you can use the GRE calculator to find the approximation of the $\sqrt{18}$, which, to the nearest hundredth, is 4.24.

Other times, however, you need an exact answer. You can use the rules of multiplying square roots to help you break down your square root into factors with perfect squares.

Check-in:

Simplify the following square roots:

1) $\sqrt{90}$ 2) $\sqrt{72}$

Solutions:

1) $\mathbf{3\sqrt{10}}$

$$\sqrt{90} = \sqrt{9} \bullet \sqrt{10} = 3 \bullet \sqrt{10} = 3\sqrt{10}$$

2) $\mathbf{6\sqrt{2}}$

$$\sqrt{72} = \sqrt{36} \bullet \sqrt{2} = 6 \bullet \sqrt{2} = 6\sqrt{2}$$
or
$$\sqrt{72} = \sqrt{9} \bullet \sqrt{8} = 3 \bullet \sqrt{8} = 3 \bullet \sqrt{4} \bullet \sqrt{2} = 3 \bullet 2 \bullet \sqrt{2} = 6\sqrt{2}$$

Adding/Subtracting Square Roots:

$$\mathbf{a\sqrt{x} + b\sqrt{x} = (a+b)\sqrt{x}}$$
$$\mathbf{a\sqrt{x} - b\sqrt{x} = (a-b)\sqrt{x}}$$

Examples:

i. $2\sqrt{3} + 5\sqrt{3} = 7\sqrt{3}$

ii. $4\sqrt{5} + 7\sqrt{5} + 2\sqrt{3} = 11\sqrt{5} + 2\sqrt{3}$

iii. $2\sqrt{18} + 5\sqrt{2} = 2 \bullet \sqrt{9} \bullet \sqrt{2} + 5\sqrt{2} = 2 \bullet 3 \bullet \sqrt{2} + 5\sqrt{2} = 6\sqrt{2} + 5\sqrt{2} = 11\sqrt{2}$

iv. $5\sqrt{2} - 2\sqrt{3}$ This expression is already simplified. Since the square square roots are different, the terms cannot be combined through subtraction.

Check-in:

Simplify the following expressions.

1. $4\sqrt{3} + 3\sqrt{3}$ 2. $4\sqrt{5} - 7\sqrt{125}$ 3. $2\sqrt{11} - 5\sqrt{2}$

Solutions:

1. $\mathbf{7\sqrt{3}}$

$4\sqrt{3} + 3\sqrt{3}$

2. $\mathbf{-31\sqrt{5}}$

$4\sqrt{5} - 7\sqrt{125} = 4\sqrt{5} - 7 \bullet \sqrt{25} \bullet \sqrt{5} = 4\sqrt{5} - 7 \bullet 5 \bullet \sqrt{5}$

$4\sqrt{5} - 7 \bullet 5 \bullet \sqrt{5} = 4\sqrt{5} - 35 \bullet \sqrt{5} = -31 \bullet \sqrt{5}$

3. $\mathbf{2\sqrt{11} - 5\sqrt{2}}$

This expression is already simplified because the square roots are different.

Rationalizing Square Roots

When square roots are in the denominator of a fraction, the fraction is considered unsimplified. To simplify, multiply the numerator and denominator by the square root in the denominator (this is called **rationalizing the denominator**). This works because the product of a square root y ($\sqrt{y}$) and itself is simply y: $\sqrt{y} \bullet \sqrt{y} = y$.

$$\frac{x}{\sqrt{y}} = \frac{x}{\sqrt{y}} \bullet \frac{\sqrt{y}}{\sqrt{y}} = \frac{x\sqrt{y}}{y}$$

Examples:

i. $\dfrac{3}{\sqrt{5}} = \dfrac{3}{\sqrt{5}} \bullet \dfrac{\sqrt{5}}{\sqrt{5}} = \dfrac{3\sqrt{5}}{5}$

ii. $\dfrac{2}{\sqrt{8}} = \dfrac{2}{2\sqrt{2}} = \dfrac{1}{\sqrt{2}} = \dfrac{1}{\sqrt{2}} \bullet \dfrac{\sqrt{2}}{\sqrt{2}} = \dfrac{\sqrt{2}}{2}$

iii. $\dfrac{6}{5\sqrt{3}} = \dfrac{6}{5\sqrt{3}} \bullet \dfrac{\sqrt{3}}{\sqrt{3}} = \dfrac{6\sqrt{3}}{5 \bullet 3} = \dfrac{6\sqrt{3}}{15} = \dfrac{2\sqrt{3}}{5}$

Check-in:

Simplify the following expressions.

1. $\dfrac{4}{\sqrt{3}}$ 2. $\dfrac{7}{\sqrt{7}}$ 3. $\dfrac{5}{2\sqrt{11}}$

Solutions:

1. $\dfrac{\mathbf{4\sqrt{3}}}{\mathbf{3}}$

$\dfrac{4}{\sqrt{3}} \bullet \dfrac{\sqrt{3}}{\sqrt{3}} = \dfrac{4\sqrt{3}}{3}$

2. $\sqrt{\mathbf{7}}$

$\dfrac{7}{\sqrt{7}} \bullet \dfrac{\sqrt{7}}{\sqrt{7}} = \dfrac{7\sqrt{7}}{7} = \sqrt{7}$

3. $\dfrac{\mathbf{5\sqrt{11}}}{\mathbf{22}}$

$\dfrac{5}{2\sqrt{11}} \bullet \dfrac{\sqrt{11}}{\sqrt{11}} = \dfrac{5\sqrt{11}}{2 \bullet 11} = \dfrac{5\sqrt{11}}{22}$

1.14 Set Notation

A **set** is a group of items, often numbers, either listed in number or expressed by rule. The following are examples of sets:

Set A= {3, 4, 5}

Set B= {2, 3, 5, 11}

Set C={3, 4}

Set D is comprised of the multiples of 5 between 10 and 30, **inclusive** (meaning, including the endpoints).

Examples of the terms defined below reference the above mentioned sets.

The **elements** (or members) of Set A are 3, 4, and 5. The elements of Set D are 10, 15, 20, 25, 30.

The **intersection** (denoted by the symbol $\cap$) of sets means those elements common to each set. For example, **Set A $\cap$ Set B** is {3, 5}.

The **union** (denoted by the symbol $\cup$) of sets means all of the elements in each set. For example: **Set A $\cup$ Set B** is {2, 3, 4, 5, 11}.

For a set to be **contained** (denoted by the symbol $\subset$) in another set, all of the elements in that set must be in the set that contains it. For example: **Set C $\subset$ Set A,** because both of the elements in Set C (3 and 4) are in Set A.

If sets have no elements in common, their intersection is the **empty set** (denoted by the symbol $\varnothing$). For example: **Set C $\cap$ Set D** is $\varnothing$, because they have no common elements.

Example 1.8

Set A= {all prime numbers}

Set B ={all even numbers}

How many elements are in the intersection of Set A and Set B?

a) 1
b) 2
c) 5
d) Infinitely many
e) None of the above

Solution:

a

Set A and Set B only have one element in common, which is the number 2. Recall that the number 2 is the only even number that is also a prime number.

CHAPTER 1 PRACTICE SET:

1) The sum of 5 consecutive integers is 35. What is the value of the greatest integer?

$$\boxed{}$$

2) What is the product of consecutive integers a, b, c, d, and e, if a<0 and e>0?

$$\boxed{}$$

3) If possible, determine which of the following is/are even, given that each variable represents an integer:

a) $2x^3y^5$

b) x+x

c) $5xyz^2$

d) 2^x, where x >0.

4)

Quantity A	Quantity B
$\dfrac{}{x}$	$\dfrac{}{x^5}$

$$x < 0$$

5)

Quantity A	Quantity B
$\dfrac{}{-|x|}$	$\dfrac{}{x}$

6)

Quantity A	Quantity B
The number of numbers between 0 and 1	The number of numbers between 1 and 5

7) Leo and Larry are not morning people. They love to hit snooze. If Leo's alarm rings every 10 minutes, beginning at 7:00 a.m., and Larry's alarm rings every 9 minutes, beginning at 8:00 a.m., at what point will their alarms ring simultaneously after Leo and Larry each have hit snooze at least once?

a) 7:30 a.m.
b) 8:00 a.m.
c) 9:15 a.m.
d) 9:30 a.m.
e) 10:30 a.m.

8) What is the smallest integer greater than 2 that leaves a remainder of 2 when divided by 3, 6, and 9?

9) If $x^4 = 81$, then what is 2^{2x}?

10) $\dfrac{\text{Quantity A}}{9^{14}}$ $\qquad$ $\dfrac{\text{Quantity B}}{3^{28}}$

11) $\dfrac{\text{Quantity A}}{27^{8}}$ $\qquad$ $\dfrac{\text{Quantity B}}{9^{14}}$

SOLUTIONS: Chapter 1 Practice Set

1) 9
2) 0
3) Even, Even, Cannot Be Determined, Even
4) d
5) c
6) c
7) d
8) 20
9) 64
10) c
11) b

EXPLANATIONS: Chapter 1 Practice Set

1) **9**

$$x + x + 1 + x + 2 + x + 3 + x + 4 = 35$$
$$5x + 10 = 35$$
$$\frac{-10}{5x} = \frac{-10}{25}$$

$$\frac{5x}{5} = \frac{25}{5}$$
$$x = 5$$

Five is the lowest integer, so the integers are 5, 6, 7, 8, and 9. Nine is the highest.

2) **0**

If there are five consecutive numbers, at least one of which is negative and at least one of which is positive—then one of them MUST be zero. (For consecutive numbers, to go from negative to positive, the list must pass through—and therefore include—zero.)

3)

a) **Even**

The product of integers is always even if at least one of them is even.

b) **Even**

x + x = 2x. Any integer times two is even.

c) **Cannot be determined.**

The only number we know for sure is 5, which is odd. Since the product of an odd and an odd is odd, and the product of an odd and an even is even, we do not know the result.

d) **Even**

The product of 2 and any integer is even. Therefore, 2 times itself any number of times is even.

4) **d**

*Remember (as mentioned on p. 15) for these types of questions the answer choices are as follows:

a: if Quantity A is always bigger
b: if Quantity B is always bigger
c: if Quantity A=Quantity B
d: if the relationship cannot be determined

Since we have no information about x, the two columns could be the same, or one could be bigger than the other. If x is zero, for example, the columns are equal. If x is greater than one, Column B is bigger. If x is between zero and one (exclusive), Column A is bigger.

5) **c**

Since both columns are based on x, they have the same absolute value. Since it is given that x<0, Column B is negative. And in Column A, the opposite of an absolute value (that isn't zero) is negative.

6) **c**

There are an infinite number of numbers between 0 and 1 and between 1 and 5. Remember, "number" does not just refer to integers!

7) **d**

The first step to solving this problem is to recognize this as a least common multiple problem: When will two things happen simultaneously?

The fact that the alarms begin at different hours is easy to take into account, since Leo's alarm will always ring on the hour. Therefore, the first time that the alarms will ring simultaneously is at 8 a.m. However, at this point, Larry hasn't had a chance to hit snooze, as his alarm is ringing now for the first time. Since the LCM of 9 and 10 is 90, so the two alarms will ring 90 minutes after 8 a.m., which is 9:30 a.m.

8) **20**

*Remember (as mentioned on p. 16) for these types of questions you must enter your answer into the solution box.**

You want to find a number that is two more (the remainder) than the least common multiple of 3, 6, and 9, which is 18. Adding 2 to 18, you get 20.

9) **64**

*Remember (as mentioned on p. 15) for these types of questions the answer choices are as follows:**

a: if Quantity A is always bigger
b: if Quantity B is always bigger
c: if Quantity A=Quantity B
d: if the relationship cannot be determined

If $x^4 = 81$, then $x = 3$, because 3^4 equals 81. The expression 2^{2x}, then, can be rewritten as $2^{2 \bullet 3}$, which is 2^6 or 64.

10) **c**

You can answer this question by manipulating Quantity A only: Since $9 = 3^2$, $9^{14} = (3^2)^{14} = 3^{28}$.

11) **b**

As in Question 10, you want to make your bases the same. In general, you want to break your larger base down to equal your smaller base so that you can compare. However, 27 is not a square or cube of 9, so you cannot break it down easily to 9. In this case, both 27 and 9 have to be broken down into a common base which in this case is 3: $27 = 3^3$ and $9 = 3^2$.

So, Column A can be rewritten as $27^8 = (3^3)^8 = 3^{24}$.

And Column B, $9^{14} = (3^2)^{14} = 3^{28}$.

Chapter 2: Not Quite Whole
(Decimals, Percents, and Fractions)

Decimals, Percents, and Fractions, oh my! These concepts are all relative to one whole. Let's start by learning how to do conversions between these three number forms.

2.1 Conversions

To convert a decimal into a fraction:

First, know your decimal places. Look at the number below and note the place value where each falls:

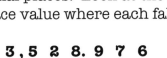

The number above is 3 thousands, 5 hundreds, 2 tens, 8 ones, 9 tenths ($\frac{9}{10}$),

7 hundredths ($\frac{7}{100}$) and 6 thousandths ($\frac{6}{1000}$).

The way you read the part of your number that falls to the right of the decimal is based on the place value that your number ends.

So, for example, if your number is .37, that is read as "37 hundredths," because your number ends in the hundredths column. Therefore, you'll write your number as $\frac{37}{100}$.

If your number is .731, it is read as "731 thousandths." You can write it as $\frac{731}{1000}$.

To convert a fraction into a decimal:

Simply divide your numerator (top number) by your denominator (bottom number) – since the fraction bar is actually a division bar—and you will get a decimal result.

For example, $\dfrac{3}{5} = 0.60$ because $3 \div 5 = 0.60$.

To convert a decimal into a percent:

Multiply by 100 by **moving your decimal two places to the right**, and add the percent sign.

For example, $0.17 = 17\%$ and $3.01 = 301\%$.

To convert a percent into a decimal:

Drop the percent sign, and divide by 100 by **moving your decimal two places to the left**.

For example, $37\% = 0.37$, $1.22\% = 0.0122$, and $801\% = 8.01$.

To convert a percent into a fraction:

Write the percent over the number 100, because percent means one-hundredth. Then reduce.

For example, $85\% = \dfrac{85}{100} = \dfrac{17}{20}$ and $3.5\% = \dfrac{3.5}{100} = \dfrac{35}{1000} = \dfrac{7}{200}$.

Phew. That's a lot of rules. Let's practice.

Check-in:

1) Convert each decimal into a percent and fraction:

a) 0.35

b) 0.078

c) 2.73

2) Convert each fraction into a decimal and percent:

a) $\dfrac{1}{5}$

b) $\dfrac{3}{12}$

c) $\dfrac{2.4}{3}$

3) Convert each percent into a decimal and fraction.

a) 73%

b) 11%

c) 161%

d) $\dfrac{5}{8}$%

4) List the following numbers in order from least to greatest:

$\dfrac{2}{3}$, 0.666, $\dfrac{5}{7}$, 66%

Solutions:

1)

a) **35% and $\dfrac{7}{20}$**

$0.35 = 35\,\%$

$0.35 = \dfrac{35}{100} = \dfrac{7}{20}$

b) **7.8% and $\dfrac{39}{500}$**

$0.078 = 7.8\%$

$0.078 = \dfrac{78}{1,000} = \dfrac{39}{500}$

c) **273% and $\dfrac{273}{100}$**

$2.73 = 273\%$

$2.73 = 2\dfrac{73}{100} = \dfrac{273}{100}$

2)

a) **0.20 and 20%**

$\dfrac{1}{5} = 0.20 = 20\%$

b) **0.25 and 25%**

$\dfrac{3}{12} = 0.25 = 25\%$

c) **0.80 and 80%**

$\dfrac{2.4}{3} = \dfrac{24}{30} = \dfrac{8}{10} = 0.80 = 80\%$

3)

a) **0.73 and $\dfrac{73}{100}$**

$$73\% = 0.73 = \frac{73}{100}$$

b) **0.11 and 11%**

$$0.11 = \frac{11}{100} = 11\%$$

c) **1.61 and $\dfrac{161}{100}$**

$$161\% = 1.61 = 1\frac{61}{100} = \frac{161}{100}$$

d) **0.00625 and $\dfrac{1}{160}$**

$$\frac{5}{8}\% = 0.625\% = .00625 = \frac{625}{100,000} = \frac{1}{160}$$

4)

$66\%, 0.666, \dfrac{2}{3}, \dfrac{5}{7}$

To answer this question, convert each answer into the same number form. In this case, decimal form is easiest.

2.2 Behaving Badly: Decimals

Decimals between zero and one, **exclusive** (meaning, not including the endpoints of zero and one) behave in the most unusual ways.

When you apply the arithmetic operations of multiplying, dividing, squaring, and square rooting to decimals, you get some very strange results:

1) When you multiply a (positive) number A by a decimal between 0 and 1, the result is SMALLER than A.

Ex: $3 \bullet .5 = 1.5$

2) When you divide a (positive) number A by a decimal between 0 and 1, the result is LARGER than A.

Ex: $\dfrac{3}{.5} = \dfrac{3}{\frac{1}{2}} = \dfrac{3}{1} \bullet \dfrac{2}{1} = 6$

3) When you take the square root of a number A between zero and one, the result is LARGER than what you started with.

Ex: $\sqrt{.49} = .70$

4) When you square a number A between zero and one, the result is SMALLER than A.

Ex: $(.2)^2 = .04$

There is sound mathematical reasoning for these rules. If it will help you remember, here it is:

Decimals between zero and one (and proper fractions) are part of a whole. So, for example, if you are squaring .5 (or ½), you are multiplying $.5 \bullet .5$. This means that you are literally taking "half (or, more generally, part) of a half"—so the result is a smaller number (in this case, a quarter—.25).

Another example: 50 • .2 means that you are taking two-tenths, or 20%, of the number 50. Since you are taking part of 50, the result must be less than 50.

> **Tip:** You can remember these rules by thinking of them as the reverse of your intuition. For example, when you multiply two positive numbers together, you generally expect the result to be larger than the inputs— but when one of them is less than one, the result is actually smaller than the larger of the original numbers. When you take the square root of a number, you generally expect that number to get smaller (ex: $\sqrt{9} = 3$), but when the number is between zero and one, the square root gets bigger instead (ex: $\sqrt{.25} = .5$).

2.2 Percents

As mentioned earlier, the word **percent** means "hundredth" or "out of 100." The key to working with percents is to realize that a percent is always relative to the whole. Consider what portion of the whole you have in order to figure out what percent you have.

To find what percent of the whole you have, simply divide what you have by the total. This will give you a decimal that you can then convert into a percent by moving the decimal point two places to the right.

Example 2.1

If you have completed 24 out of 30 problems in a practice set, what percent have you completed?

Solution:

80%

The fractional part completed is $\dfrac{24}{30}$.

Divide 24 by 30. You get .8. Move the decimal two places to the right to get 80%:

$$\frac{24}{30} = .8 = 80\%$$

Example 2.2

Luke completed x out of y problems in a practice set. What percent did he complete?

Solution:

$$\frac{100x}{y}\%$$

As in Example 2.1, divide x by y. To convert the resulting fraction into a percent, multiply by 100 (which is the equivalent of moving the decimal two places to the right).

$$\frac{x}{y} = \frac{100x}{y}\%$$

Another important concept regarding percents is percent change. The **percent change** of a number A to a number B is found by calculating the difference between the two numbers (A - B), relative to the base number (A):

$$\textbf{Percent Change} = \frac{100 \bullet (\text{Difference})}{\text{Base}}$$

The key to percent change is understanding that you are finding the change relative to a base amount. It is important to be able to identify both the change and the reference amount.

Note: The "100" that you are multiplying by in the formula converts your decimal result into a percent. Since percent is 1/100, the percent sign cancels out multiplying by 100.

Note: If you decrease a number by a certain percent, you must increase the result by a GREATER percent in order to return it to its original value.

Example 2.3a

Garrett bought a house for $125,000, and sold the house 12 years later for $150,000. What was the percent increase?

Solution:

The change in cost was $25,000, so that's the difference. And the base (or original number) is $125,000, so:

$$\text{Percent Change} = \frac{100 \cdot (150,000 - 125,000)}{125,000} = \frac{2,500,000}{125,000} = 20\%$$

Example 2.3b

Garrett bought a house for $150,000, and sold the house in a down market for $125,000. What was the percent decrease?

Solution:

Again, the change in cost was $25,000. This time, however, the base number is larger— $150,000.

$$\text{Percent Change} = \frac{100 \cdot (150,000 - 125,000)}{150,000} = \frac{2,500,000}{150,000} = 16\frac{2}{3}\%$$

Notice that Examples 2.3a and 2.3b are very similar. The difference between the two problems is that the original cost of the house and the new cost of the house were switched. The change between the two numbers in both examples is $25,000. However, $25,000 is a bigger percent of $125,000 than $25,000 is of $150,000.

Example 2.4

One column of data on a spreadsheet was accidentally input at 30% below their original values. To the nearest tenth of a percent, by what percent must the value be increased to correct this error (meaning, to return the data to their proper values)?

Solution:

Let's say that one of your data values should have been 100. The mistaken value, then, is shown to be 70. You must increase your data value to 100, which is a difference of 30, in order to restore it to its proper value. Find the percent change by using the formula:

$$\text{Percent Change} = \frac{100 \cdot \text{Difference}}{\text{Base}} = \frac{100(100-70)}{70} = 42.9\%$$

If you prefer to solve this directly, let the intended input be represented by x. The data, then, was accidentally input at 70%x. To correct the error by changing the data to x (which is 100%x), find the percent increase from 70%x to 100%x:

$$\text{Percent Change} = \frac{100 \cdot (100\%x - 70\%x)}{70\%x} = \frac{100 \cdot (30\%x)}{70\%x} = \frac{100 \cdot (.30x)}{.70x} = \frac{30x}{.70x}$$

$$\frac{30x}{.70x} = 42.9\%$$

Think about it: Always ask yourself, does my answer make sense? In this case: If I raise 70 by 30, does it seem reasonable that this results in a 42.9% increase? Well, if I were to raise 70 by 35, that would be a 50% increase—so yes, finding 30 to be 42.9% of 70 is reasonable.

2.3 Fractions

"Ugh. Can't we just skip fractions?" Sorry, no can do. But really, fractions are not that bad! A fraction is simply a part relative to its whole. So, if you buy a six-pack of bagels, and eat 5 of them, you have eaten 5 out of 6 or 5/6 of your bagels. And you have 1 out of 6 or 1/6 of your bagels left.

flummox (flum'əks) vt. [Old Slang] to confuse; perplex

The top number of the fraction is the numerator (the part); the bottom number is the denominator (the whole).:

$$\frac{\text{Numerator}}{\text{Denominator}}$$

The **reciprocal** of a number is used to help you simplify expressions and solve equations.

The **reciprocal** is the inversion of the numerator and denominator, found by simply inverting the numerator and the denominator of your fraction. So, for example, the reciprocal of $\frac{3}{4}$ is $\frac{4}{3}$.

The product of a number and its reciprocal is 1:

$$\frac{3}{4} \bullet \frac{4}{3} = 1$$

Check-in: Find the reciprocal of the following:

a) $\frac{2}{3}$ b) $\frac{7}{5}$ c) 3

Solution:

a) $\frac{3}{2}$ b) $\frac{5}{7}$ c) $\frac{1}{3}$

Note that, as in answer choice c, any integer can be written as a fraction by placing it over the number one $\frac{3}{1}$. Then you can take the reciprocal of the resulting fraction.

2.4 Equivalent Fractions and Reducing Fractions

Fractions are considered **equivalent** if they have the same value. In order to determine if fractions are equivalent, you can simplify them by reducing them.

To reduce fractions:

Divide the numerator and denominator by their greatest common factor. (If you are not sure what the greatest common factor is, divide by the largest or easiest one you know. Then continue to divide by common factors.) For example, if you have the fraction 6/8, you will notice that both the numerator and denominator are multiples of 2. Therefore, you can divide both your numerator and denominator by 2 to get 3/4.

> **Remember:** Whatever you divide (or multiply) the numerator of your fraction by, you must divide (or multiply) the denominator by in order to maintain an equivalent value.

Check-in: Reduce the following fractions:

a) $\frac{5}{15}$ b) $\frac{36}{84}$ c) $\frac{48}{12}$

Solution:

a) $\frac{1}{3}$ b) $\frac{3}{7}$ c) 4

Note: In Check-in problem part b, it might not immediately be clear that you can divide the numerator and denominator by 12. But it should be clear that you can divide by 2 since both numbers are even. Once you divide by 2, you'll notice that you can continue to divide. It is fine (albeit, potentially time consuming) to simplify your fractions in stages.

2.5 Operations With Fractions

To add and subtract fractions:

You must get a **common denominator**. A **common denominator** is simply a common multiple of your denominators. To keep the numbers small, you can find the least common multiple among your denominators.

For example, to add $\dfrac{2}{11}$ and $\dfrac{3}{7}$, first find the least common denominator, which is 77. $\dfrac{2}{11}$ can be rewritten as $\dfrac{14}{77}$ and $\dfrac{3}{7}$ can be rewritten as $\dfrac{33}{77}$:

$$\frac{2}{11}+\frac{3}{7}=\frac{2\bullet 7}{11\bullet 7}+\frac{3\bullet 11}{7\bullet 11}=\frac{14}{77}+\frac{33}{77}=\frac{47}{77}$$

Check-in:

a) $\dfrac{1}{5}+\dfrac{2}{3}$ b) $\dfrac{4}{7}+\dfrac{2}{9}$ c) $\dfrac{5}{8}-\dfrac{1}{4}$

Solution:

a) $\dfrac{13}{15}$

The common denominator between 5 and 3 is 15. Therefore, both denominators must be changed to 15. The number you multiply a denominator by to get to 15, you must also multiply the numerator by:

$$\frac{1}{5}+\frac{2}{3} = \frac{1\bullet3}{5\bullet3}+\frac{2\bullet5}{3\bullet5} = \frac{3}{15}+\frac{10}{15}=\frac{13}{15}$$

b) $\dfrac{\mathbf{50}}{\mathbf{63}}$

$$\frac{4}{7}+\frac{2}{9} = \frac{4\bullet9}{7\bullet9}+\frac{2\bullet7}{9\bullet7}=\frac{36}{63}+\frac{14}{63}=\frac{50}{63}$$

c) $\dfrac{\mathbf{3}}{\mathbf{8}}$

$$\frac{5}{8}-\frac{1}{4} = \frac{5}{8}-\frac{1\bullet2}{4\bullet2} = \frac{5}{8}-\frac{2}{8}=\frac{3}{8}$$

Note in this case that the common denominator is 8, so the first fraction does not need to be changed.

Multiplying fractions:

To multiply fractions, simply multiply across: Multiply the numerators to get your new numerator and multiply the denominators to get your new denominator.

For example, $\dfrac{2}{11}\bullet\dfrac{3}{7}=\dfrac{2\bullet3}{11\bullet7}=\dfrac{6}{77}$.

When possible, you can reduce your fractions before multiplying. This will allow you to work with smaller numbers. Any numerator can be reduced with any denominator that is being multiplied together, given that they have common factors.

Check-in:

a) $\dfrac{1}{5}\bullet\dfrac{2}{3}$ b) $\dfrac{4}{7}\bullet\dfrac{14}{9}$ c) $\dfrac{5}{8}\bullet\dfrac{1}{4}$

63

Solution:

a) $\dfrac{2}{15}$

b) $\dfrac{8}{9}$

Note that the 14 in the second numerator can reduce with the 7 in the first denominator. After you reduce, note that the 14 is replaced by a 2 and the 7 is replaced by a 1.

If you don't reduce as you go along, you can reduce at the end: Multiplying the fractions together, you get 56/63. Both the top and bottom are divisible by 7, so your answer reduces to 8/9.

c) $\dfrac{5}{32}$

To divide fractions:

To divide fractions, multiply the first fraction by the **reciprocal** of the second fraction.

For example, $\dfrac{\dfrac{2}{11}}{\dfrac{3}{7}} = \dfrac{2}{11} \bullet \dfrac{7}{3} = \dfrac{14}{33}$.

Check-in:

a) $\dfrac{\dfrac{1}{5}}{\dfrac{2}{3}}$ b) $\dfrac{\dfrac{4}{7}}{\dfrac{14}{9}}$ c) $\dfrac{5}{8} \div 3$

Solution:

a) $\dfrac{\mathbf{3}}{\mathbf{10}}$

$$\frac{\frac{1}{5}}{\frac{2}{3}} = \frac{1}{5} \bullet \frac{3}{2} = \frac{3}{10}$$

b) $\dfrac{\mathbf{18}}{\mathbf{49}}$

$$\frac{\frac{4}{7}}{\frac{14}{9}} = \frac{4}{7} \bullet \frac{9}{14} = \frac{18}{49}$$

c) $\dfrac{\mathbf{5}}{\mathbf{24}}$

$$\frac{5}{8} \div 3 = \frac{5}{8} \div \frac{3}{1} = \frac{5}{8} \bullet \frac{1}{3} = \frac{5}{24}$$

2.6 Improper Fractions and Mixed Numbers

Improper fractions are fractions in which the absolute value of the numerator is greater than that of the denominator. The absolute values of these fractions are greater than one.

You can add, subtract, multiply, and divide improper fractions just as you would any other fraction.

In addition, improper fractions can be turned into mixed numbers, and vice versa. A mixed number is a number that is comprised of both an integer and a fraction, like $1\frac{1}{2}$ and $2\frac{3}{4}$. Respectively, these numbers are just another way of writing $1 + \frac{1}{2}$ and $2 + \frac{3}{4}$.

To perform operations with mixed numbers, it is often easiest to first change them into improper fractions:

Since $1\frac{1}{2}$ is $1 + \frac{1}{2}$, simply get a common denominator and add the fractions:

$$1 + \frac{1}{2} = \frac{1}{1} + \frac{1}{2} = \frac{2}{2} + \frac{1}{2} = \frac{3}{2}.$$

The shortcut to changing a mixed number into an improper fraction is often taught in grade school: Multiply the integer by the denominator and add it to the numerator. This is your new numerator. Place this numerator on top of the denominator:

$$3\frac{1}{2} = \frac{3 \bullet 2 + 1}{2} = \frac{7}{2}.$$

Check-in:

a) $1\frac{1}{5} + 3\frac{5}{8}$ b) $2\frac{1}{4} + \frac{1}{3}$

Solution:

a) $4\frac{33}{40}$

$$1\frac{1}{5} + 3\frac{5}{8} = \frac{6}{5} + \frac{29}{8} = \frac{48}{40} + \frac{145}{40} = \frac{193}{40} = 4\frac{33}{40}$$

Alternatively, add the integers and the fractions separately:

$$1\frac{1}{5} + 3\frac{5}{8} = 1 + 3 + \frac{1}{5} + \frac{5}{8} = 4 + \frac{8}{40} + \frac{25}{40} = 4\frac{33}{40}$$

b) $2\frac{7}{12}$

$$2\frac{1}{4} + \frac{1}{3} = 2 + \frac{1}{4} + \frac{1}{3} = 2 + \frac{3}{12} + \frac{4}{12} = 2\frac{7}{12}$$

To change an improper fraction into a mixed number:

Divide the numerator by the denominator, and write the remainder over the denominator:

Example: $\dfrac{5}{3}$ = $3\overline{)5}$ $^{1\,R.\,2}$ = $1\dfrac{2}{3}$

Now try your hand at a couple of word problems involving fractions. And, just a head's up, you're not seeing double in Example 2.5 a and Example 2.5 b. Notice the subtle difference in wording between them.

Example 2.5a

Clara spent $\dfrac{1}{3}$ of her salary on housing expenses and $\dfrac{1}{10}$ of her salary on food. What fractional part of her salary did she have left after paying for her housing and food?

Solution:

$\dfrac{17}{30}$

Clara spent $\dfrac{1}{3} + \dfrac{1}{10}$ of her salary on housing and food expenses, respectively, which is $\dfrac{13}{30}$ of her salary. Therefore, she has $1 - \dfrac{13}{30}$, or $\dfrac{17}{30}$ of her salary left. (The reason we subtract the expenses from the value "1" is that the "1"

represents one full salary.)

Example 2.5 b

Clara spent $\dfrac{1}{3}$ of her salary on housing expenses and $\dfrac{1}{10}$ of the remainder on food. What fractional part of her salary did she have left after paying for her housing and food?

Solution:

$$\frac{3}{5}$$

Clara spent $\frac{1}{3}$ of her salary on housing expenses, which means she had $\frac{2}{3}$ of her salary left. She then spent $\frac{1}{10}$ of $\frac{2}{3}$ of her salary on food, which is $\frac{2}{30}$ (or reduced, $\frac{1}{15}$) of her salary on food. Between food and housing expenses, she spent $\frac{1}{15} + \frac{1}{3}$ of her salary, which adds to $\frac{6}{15}$ (or, reduced, $\frac{2}{5}$). Therefore, she has $\frac{9}{15}$, or $\frac{3}{5}$ of her salary remaining.

CHAPTER 2 PRACTICE SET:

1) Nico applied for 120 jobs. If he was offered first round interviews for half of them, and second round interviews for 10% of the first round interviews, how many total interview offers did he receive?

a) 60

b) 66

c) 72

d) 80

e) 88

2) Initially, Kevin sold three quarters of his hot peppers at the Farmer's Market. Not wanting to take his peppers back home, he cut the price in half and sold one fifth of the remaining peppers during the last hour. What percent of Kevin's peppers did he have to take back home?

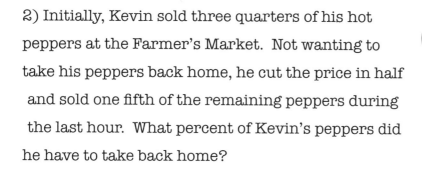

a) 0.05%
b) 0.20%
c) 5.0%
d) 20.0%
e) None of the above

3) At the same Farmer's Market, Becca initially sold two thirds of her produce. At the end of the day, she took Kevin's lead and decided to cut her prices in half. This resulted in her selling another 20 percent of her goods. If she had sold her entire inventory at full price, she would have grossed $x. Instead, how much did she gross (in terms of x)?

a) $\dfrac{1}{83}x$

b) $\dfrac{23}{30}x$

c) $\dfrac{13}{15}x$

d) $\dfrac{11}{12}x$

e) $\dfrac{83}{100}x$

4) List the following numbers in order from least to greatest:

$.4, \dfrac{4}{7}, .42\%, \dfrac{4}{9}, .39$

a) $\dfrac{4}{7}, .42\%, \dfrac{4}{9}, .39, .4$

b) $.42\%, .39, .4, \dfrac{4}{9}, \dfrac{4}{7}$

c) $.39, .4, .42\%, \dfrac{4}{9}, \dfrac{4}{7}$

d) $\dfrac{4}{7}, \dfrac{4}{9}, .39, .4, .42\%$

e) $.42\%, .4, .39, \dfrac{4}{9}, \dfrac{4}{7}$

5) Taylor lost 8 pounds. If this represents 5% of her original weight, how many pounds does she now weigh?

a) 140

b) 146

c) 150

d) 152

e) 160

6) Carlos spent 85% of his paycheck. If he has $30 left, what was the amount of his check?

a) $35

b) $115

c) $200

d) $270

e) $300

7) If 12% of a number is 32, what is 60% of that number?

8) Reggie's room was a mess. After cleaning it up, he was able to find 80% of his baseball cards. If he was still missing 12 cards, how many had he found?

9)

Quantity A	Quantity B
40% of 20% of 12	8% of 150% of 16

SOLUTIONS: Chapter 2 Practice Set

1) b
2) d
3) b
4) b
5) d
6) c
7) 160
8) 48
9) b

EXPLANATIONS: Chapter 2 Practice Set

1) **b**

Nico initially received 60 interviews. Of these 60 interviews, he received 10% (which is 6) additional interviews for round two.

2) **d**

Kevin ultimately sold 80% of his hot peppers, so he had to take the other 20% home:

He initially sold 75% (or $\frac{3}{4}$), and then sold $\frac{1}{5}$ of the remaining 25%

(which is $\frac{1}{5} \cdot 25\% = \frac{1}{5} \cdot \frac{25}{100} = \frac{1}{5} \cdot \frac{1}{4} = \frac{1}{20} = .05 = 5\%$). So, in total he sold 75% + 5% = 80%.

Thus, he took 20% home.

3) **b**

Becca initially sold $\frac{2}{3}$ of her produce at full price, grossing $\frac{2}{3} \cdot x$,

and then another 20% at half price, grossing ($20\% \cdot \frac{1}{2} \cdot x$ or $\frac{1}{10} \cdot x$).

Add $\frac{2}{3}x$ and $\frac{1}{10}x$ to get $\frac{23}{30}x$, her gross revenue.

4) **b**

To answer this question, convert every number to the same form. In this case, it is easiest to convert each number to a decimal. Put 4/9 and 4/7 into your calculator to get their decimal equivalents. Also, note that .42% has a decimal in front of it, so its value is .0042.

5) **d**

Use the percent change formula:
$$\frac{100 \cdot (\text{Difference})}{\text{Base}}$$

Given that the change in weight is 8 pounds and the original weight is unknown:

$$\frac{(100)8}{x} = 5$$

$$5x = 800$$

$$\frac{5x}{5} = \frac{800}{5}$$

$$x = 160$$

Taylor now weighs 160-8 = 152 pounds.

6) **c**

Carlos' $30 remaining represents 15% of the original:

$$30 = .15x$$

$$\frac{30}{.15} = \frac{.15x}{.15}$$

$$x = 200$$

Carlos originally had $200.

7) **160**

$$.12x = 32$$

$$\frac{.12x}{.12} = \frac{32}{.12}$$

$$x = 266\frac{2}{3}$$

$$.60x = .60(266\frac{2}{3}) = 160$$

Alternatively:

60% is 5 times 12%, so multiply 32 by 5 to get 160.

8) **48**

Twelve (12) of Reggie's cards are missing, which is 20% of the total cards. Let x represent the total number of cards:

12 = 0.20x

$$\frac{12}{.20} = \frac{.20x}{.20}$$

x = 60

60 is the total, but Reggie only found 48 because 12 are still missing.

9) **b**

Quantity A   .4 • .2 • 12 = .96   Quantity B   .08 • 1.5 • 16 = 1.92

Chapter 3: Things Will Balance Out
(Ratios and Proportions)

To make margaritas—or so we're told—you need 6 ounces of tequila for every 5 cups of ice. This is a ratio telling you how many parts of one ingredient you need for a certain number of parts of another ingredient. According to the recipe, if you use these quantities, you will be able to make 4 servings. But let's say you want to make 8 servings. How much tequila and ice would you need then?

That's right—12 ounces of tequila and 10 cups of ice. In order to double your servings you need to double each of the ingredients. Despite doubling the recipe, you'll notice that the balance remains the same.

That's what ratios tell you—the amount of one thing you have relative to another. It doesn't tell you an absolute number—only a relative number. So, if you have a ratio of 3 to 2, you know that for every 3 parts of one thing you have, you have 2 parts of another.

3.1 Ratios

A **ratio** is a comparison of two (or more) parts. For example, if there are 3 girls and 5 boys:

—the ratio of girls to boys is 3:5,

—the ratio of boys to girls is 5:3, and

—the ratio of boys to all children is 5:8.

The last example— the ratio of boys to all children— is also a **fraction**. Fractions compare parts to its whole (which is the sum of its parts), whereas ratios generally compare parts to parts.

For example, if the ratio of green to blue to yellow marbles is 5: 7: 9, respectively, each number represents a "part." The whole (or total number of parts) is 5+7+9, or 21 parts.

The fractional part of all marbles that is green, for example, is $\frac{5}{21}$.

A ratio can be expressed as $a : b$, a to b, or $\dfrac{a}{b}$.

Note that fractions and ratios can both be written in fraction form, so you have to pay attention to the context of the problem.

Example 3.1

If the ratio of apples to oranges in the cafeteria is 5:8 respectively, which of the following could be the total number of apples and oranges in the cafeteria? (Indicate all that apply.)

a) 13

b) 26

c) 40

d) 65

e) 80

f) 143

Solution:

a, b, d, and f

We know that for every 5 apples there are 8 oranges. This means that one complete set of apples and oranges is 13 pieces of fruit (5+8). Since we can have multiple sets of fruit, any multiple of 13 works.

Example 3.2

If 25% of c equals 60% of e, what is the ratio of c to e?

a) 5:12

b) 5:7

c) 7:12

d) 12:5

e) 12:7

Solution:

d

Keep in mind that you are asked to find:

$c : e$ or $\dfrac{c}{e}$

You are given 25%c=60%e. Solve for c (or e):

$0.25c = 0.60e$

$$\dfrac{0.25c}{0.25} = \dfrac{0.60e}{0.25}$$

$c = 2.4e$

Therefore, substituting 2.4e in for c :

$c : e = 2.4e : e$

    $= 2.4 \ : \ 1$ Divide both sides of the ratio by e

    $= 24 \ \ :10$ Multiply both sides of the ratio by 10 to get rid of decimal

    $=12 \ \ : \ 5$ Simplify

Rates

A **rate** is a type of ratio that compares two measurements of different units. Examples include: miles per hour, miles per gallon, feet per minute, dollars per hour.

Example 3.3

Meghan drove 135 miles in 3 hours and Noelle drove 160 miles in 4 hours.
How many miles per hour faster did Meghan drive than Noelle?

a) 5

b) 10

c) 15

d) 40

e) 45

Solution:

a

Meghan's rate was $\dfrac{135\,m}{3\,h}$, which reduces to 45 miles per hour. Noelle's

rate was $\dfrac{160\,m}{4\,h}$, which reduces to 40 miles per hour. Therefore, the

difference in their driving rates was 5 miles per hour.

Example 3.4

Meghan drove x miles in y hours and Noelle drove y miles in x hours,
where x>y. What is the positive difference in their driving speeds?

a) $x - y$

b) $y - x$

c) $\dfrac{y - x}{xy}$

d) $\dfrac{y^2 - x^2}{xy}$

e) $\dfrac{x^2 - y^2}{xy}$

Solution:

e

This is a similar example to 3.3, but the value of the distance and time traveled of each woman are not known. This can be solved directly or indirectly.

Directly:

Meghan's rate was $\dfrac{x}{y}$ miles per hour. Noelle's rate was $\dfrac{y}{x}$ miles per hour.

Since x>y, Meghan's rate was faster than Noelle's. Subtract their rates, making sure that Meghan's rate goes before Noelle's rate in the problem, so that the difference is positive:

$$\frac{x}{y} - \frac{y}{x}$$

Find a common denominator, which is xy:

$$\frac{x}{y} - \frac{y}{x} = \frac{x \bullet x}{xy} - \frac{y \bullet y}{xy} = \frac{x^2 - y^2}{xy}$$

Indirectly:

Choose a value for x and a value for y, making sure that they meet the condition that x>y.

For example, let x = 6 and y = 2. That makes Meghan's rate $\dfrac{6}{2}$ miles / hour (reducing to $\dfrac{3}{1}$) and Noelle's rate is $\dfrac{2}{6}$ miles / hour (reducing to $\dfrac{1}{3}$).

Now subtract the two rates:

$$\frac{3}{1} - \frac{1}{3} = \frac{3 \bullet 3}{1 \bullet 3} - \frac{1}{3} = \frac{9}{3} - \frac{1}{3} = \frac{8}{3}$$

So, when x = 6 and y = 2, the positive difference between Meghan's and Noelle's rates is $\frac{8}{3}$.

The final step, then, is to plug in x = 6 and y = 2 in to each of the answer choices to find the one that gives you $\frac{8}{3}$.

Note: Choosing numbers is a particularly time consuming process. If more than one answer choice results in $\frac{8}{3}$, you have to go back to the beginning and choose different values for x and y, repeating the entire process (even though you only plug in values for the answer choices that worked the last time, not for the ones that didn't result in $\frac{8}{3}$).

Extended Ratios

Consider the following example:

The ratio of a:b = 3:5. The ratio of b:c = 5:11. What is the ratio of a:c?

(If you got 3:11, good job!)

In this case, the ratios can be combined to get a:b:c = 3:5:11. This is possible because b is repeated in both ratios AND the value of b is the same in each ratio.

Now, consider the following:

The ratio of a:b = 3:5. The ratio of b:c= 4:7. What is the ratio of a:c?
In this case, you CANNOT simply say 3:7, because the value of the variable

present in each ratio (which is b) is different in each ratio. In the first ratio, b is 5 and in the second, b is 4. In order to make a and c comparable, you must first make the b values the same.

Thus, we need to change the b into a number that is a common multiple of both the 4 and the 5 (in this case, 20 works). Just remember that, like an equation, whatever you do to one side of a ratio you must do the other. Therefore, we have to multiply both sides of the first ratio by 4 and both sides of the second ratio by 5.

The result:

a:b = 3:5 becomes a:b = 12:20 and b:c = 4:7 becomes b:c= 20:35.

Thus, the ratio of a:c= 12:35.

Example 3.5

If the ratio of lugs to bugs is 2 to 5, and the ratio of bugs to fugs is 3 to 7, what is the ratio of lugs to fugs?

Solution:

6:35

Since "bugs" is common to both ratios, these values need to be the same. Change the value of bugs in each ratio to 15 (a multiple common to both 3 and 5). This requires you to multiply both sides of the first ratio by 3 and both sides of the second ratio by 5:

lugs: bugs = 2:5 becomes lugs: bugs = 6:15 (after multiplying both sides by 3), and

bugs:fugs = 3:7 becomes bugs: fugs=15:35 (after multiplying both sides by 5).

Since the new forms of the ratios are now comparable, we can see that the ratio of lugs to fugs is 6:35.

Example 3.6

If the ratio of a to b is 3 to 5, and the ratio of b to c is 7 to 9, what is the ratio of c to a?

a) 3:5

b) 5:7

c) 7:9

d) 9:15

e) 15:7

Solution:

e

$a:b = 3:5$	Given
$b:c = 7:9$	
$c:a = ?:?$	Find
$a:b = 21:35$	Find the LCM of 5 and 7 (which is 35) and re-write
$b:c = 35:45$	each ratio as equivalent ratios
$c:a = 45:21$	Now that the b values are the same, c and a can be directly compared
$c:a = 15:7$	Reduce

3.2 Proportions

C'Mon, man, let's not blow things out of...

Proportions are two equal rates or ratios:

$$\frac{a}{b} = \frac{c}{d}$$

Setting up and solving proportions allow us to solve for unknown measurements and quantities.

To solve a proportion, set equivalent ratios equal to each other and **cross-multiply.** That is:

$$\boxed{\text{If } \frac{a}{b} = \frac{c}{d}, \text{ then } a \bullet d = b \bullet c.}$$

When you solve a proportion, you will generally have three out of four inputs, which you will use to find the fourth.

Check-in:

Solve for the variable.

1) $\dfrac{6}{5} = \dfrac{12}{y}$ 2) $\dfrac{x+3}{9} = \dfrac{1}{5}$

Solutions:

1) **y = 10**

$$\frac{6}{5} = \frac{12}{y}$$

$$6 \bullet y = 5 \bullet 12$$

$$6y = 60$$

$$\frac{6y}{6} = \frac{60}{6}$$

$$y = 10$$

2) **x = $\frac{-6}{5}$**

$$\frac{x+3}{9} = \frac{1}{5}$$

$$5(x+3) = 1 \bullet 9$$

$$5x + 15 = 9 \qquad \text{Distribute}$$

$$5x + 15 = 9$$

$$\underline{\quad -15 \quad -15\quad}$$

$$5x = -6$$

$$\frac{5x}{5} = \frac{-6}{5}$$

$$x = \frac{-6}{5}$$

84

When setting up proportions, it is key to compare **"like to like."**
Follow the examples below, which illustrate this point.

Example 3.7

Damon gets $50 for every 7 magazine subscriptions he sells. If Damon sells 84 magazine subscriptions, how much money will he make?

Solution:

$600

$$\frac{\$50}{7} = \frac{\$x}{84}$$

Notice that we are comparing like to like. The money Damon makes relative to selling 7 subscriptions is proportional to the money he makes relative to selling 84 subscriptions.

When we cross-multiply, we get:

$$\$50 \bullet 84 = 7x$$

$$\frac{\$50 \bullet 84}{7} = \frac{7x}{7}$$

$$\$600 = x$$

Example 3.8

Returning to the margarita example from the chapter's opening, to make 4 servings of margaritas, you need six ounces of tequila for every five cups of ice. How much tequila would you need to make 7 servings?

Solution:

10.5 ounces of tequila

$$\frac{4\text{ servings}}{6\text{ ounces}} = \frac{7\text{ servings}}{x\text{ ounces}}$$

Note : Both sides of the equation have numerators measured in servings and denominators measured in ounces.

Next, cross multiply :

$$4x = 6 \bullet 7$$

$$4x = 42$$

$$\frac{4x}{4} = \frac{42}{4}$$

$$x = 10.5$$

Example 3.9

Nickels Nursery School requires 3 chaperones for every 5 toddlers who go on a field trip.

a) If 15 toddlers are going on the trip, how many chaperones are needed?

b) If 5 chaperones volunteer to go on the trip, how many toddlers can go?

c) If 12 chaperones are needed for the trip, what is the minimum number of toddlers expected to go?

Solution:

a) **9**

$$\frac{3}{5} = \frac{x}{15}$$ Set up a proportion, comparing like to like.

$$45 = 5x$$ Cross multiply.

$$9 = x$$

b) **8**

$$\frac{3}{5} = \frac{5}{x}$$

$$3x = 25$$

$$\frac{3x}{3} = \frac{25}{3}$$

$$x = \frac{25}{3} = 8\frac{1}{3}$$

At most, 8 toddlers can go (since we can't take part of a toddler!).

c) **19**

Following the same process as a) and b), with 11 chaperones, we see that 18 toddlers can be accommodated. Therefore, the 19th toddler requires an additional chaperone, for a total of 12 chaperones.

This one is trickier than the others: If you cross-multiplied with an input of 12 chaperones, you would find that 20 toddlers can be accommodated. While this is true, this is the maximum, not the **minimum,** number of toddlers who can be accommodated given that 12 chaperones are required.

Example 3.10

Find the value of x in terms of y, if:

$$\frac{x + y}{y} = \frac{7}{3}$$

Solution:

$$x = \frac{4y}{3}$$

Note, to solve for a variable x "in terms of y," simply means to solve for x. The phrase, "in terms of y" is used because the solution will have a y in it. Start by cross-multiplying the given information to get the problem out of fraction form:

$$\frac{x + y}{y} = \frac{7}{3}$$

$$3(x+y) = 7 \bullet y$$

$3x + 3y = 7y$ (Note that the entire numerator is multiplied by 3.)

$$\frac{-3y \quad -3y}{3x \quad = 4y}$$

$$\frac{3x}{3} = \frac{4y}{3}$$

$$x = \frac{4y}{3}$$

CHAPTER 3 PRACTICE SET:

1) Sonya is having a dinner party for eight. The recipe she is using makes five servings. By what percent must she increase the recipe to allow for partygoers to have two servings each?

a) 100%

b) 120%

c) 220%

d) 300%

e) 320%

2) If the ratio of strawberry to vanilla to chocolate ice cream sold at Yummy's Ice Creamery is 5:8:11, respectively, what is the ratio of ice cream sold that is NOT chocolate to all ice cream?

a) 5:8

b) 13:24

c) 8:5

d) 13:8

e) 24:13

3) If $\frac{2}{3}$ of the women at the conference are entrepreneurs, what is the ratio of women who are not entrepreneurs to women who are entrepreneurs?

a) 1:3

b) 1:2

c) 2:3

d) 2:1

e) 3:1

4) If the ratio of winning tickets to losing tickets is 1:5, and 360 of the tickets are not winning tickets, how many total tickets are there?

```
┌─────────────┐
│             │
│             │
└─────────────┘
```

5) Ike spent twice as much time biking as walking, and three times as much time walking as swimming. What is the ratio of the time Ike spent biking to the time he spent swimming?

a) 1:6

b) 1:3

c) 1:2

d) 2:1

e) 6:1

6) For a school play, if the ratio of the cost of children's tickets to adults' tickets was 1 to 2, and the ratio of the number of children's tickets sold to adults' tickets sold was 3 to 1, what fractional part of the ticket sale revenue can be attributed to the sale of children's tickets?

```
┌─────────────┐
│             │
│             │
└─────────────┘
```

7) On a map of Adler's Amusement Park, Wily's Waterslide is 3.5 inches from the Demented Drop Rollercoaster. The map's key says that 1/4 inch represents 200 feet. How far apart is the waterslide from the rollercoaster (in feet)?

a) 700

b) 950

c) 1,600

d) 2,200

e) 2,800

8) Alex took a speed reading class. She can read 12 pages in 45 seconds. At this rate, how many minutes will it take her to read 90 pages (to the nearest minute)?

a) 5

b) 6

c) 7

d) 8

e) 9

9) Alex's brother Sam took the same speed reading class. He also can read 12 pages in 45 seconds. At this rate, how many minutes will it take him to read x pages?

a) $\dfrac{x}{16}$

b) $\dfrac{x}{12}$

c) $\dfrac{9x}{16}$

d) $\dfrac{3x}{4}$

e) 16x

10) If it takes 2/3 of an hour to drive 80 miles, driving at the same rate, how many minutes will it take to drive 120 miles?

a) 1

b) 30

c) 60

d) 75

e) 90

11) On average, John can make 12 free throws in two minutes. If he maintains his average by making x free throws, how many minutes has he been shooting?

a) $\dfrac{x}{12}$

b) $\dfrac{12}{x}$

c) $6x$

d) $\dfrac{x}{6}$

e) $\dfrac{6}{x}$

SOLUTIONS: Chapter 3 Practice Set

1) c
2) b
3) b
4) 432
5) e
6) $\dfrac{3}{5}$
7) e
8) b
9) a
10) c
11) d

EXPLANATIONS: Chapter 3 Practice Set

1) **c**

In order to have enough for each partygoer to have two servings, Sonya must make 16 servings. The recipe only serves 5. To figure out the increase in percent from 5 to 16, use the percent change formula.

$$\text{Percent Change} = \frac{100\,(\text{Difference})}{\text{Base}} = \frac{100\,(16-5)}{5} = \frac{1100}{5} = 220$$

2) **b**

Since this is a ratio problem, each number represents the number of parts of ice cream. There are 24 total parts: 5+8+11, 13 of which (5+8) are not chocolate.

3) **b**

If 2/3 of the women at the conference are entrepreneurs, then 1/3 of the women are NOT entrepreneurs. The ratio of women who are not entrepreneurs to women who are entrepreneurs, then, is $1/3 : 2/3$. In order to simplify this ratio (since ratios are represented in whole numbers), multiply both sides of the ratio by 3:

$$\frac{1}{3} \bullet 3 : \frac{2}{3} \bullet 3$$

1:2

4) **432**

Since the ratio of winning tickets to losing tickets is 1:5, and 360 of the

93

tickets are not winning tickets, the following proportion allows you to find the number of winning tickets:

$$\frac{1}{5} = \frac{x}{360}$$

$5x = 360$ Cross multiply

$$\frac{5x}{5} = \frac{360}{5}$$ Divide both sides by 5

$x = 72$

The total number of tickets can be found by adding the winning and non-winning tickets: $72 + 360 = 432$.

5) **e**

The ratio of time spent biking to time spent walking is b:w = 2:1, and the ratio of time spent walking to time spent swimming is w:s= 3:1.

The common type of exercise to both ratios is walking, so those values must be the same. The common multiple between the two different walking values is 3, so change the first ratio accordingly:

b:w= 2:1 becomes b:w= 6:3 (multiply both sides of the ratio by 3)

w:s= 3:1 (There is no need to change this ratio, as the parts spent walking is already "3".)

Thus, the ratio of b:s= 6:1.

Alternatively:

If b = time spent biking, w = time spent walking, and s = time spent swimming,

then b = 2w and w = 3s.

Solve for both b and s in terms of w. (This way the "w"s cancel out.)

Since w = 3s, dividing both sides by 3: $s = \dfrac{w}{3}$.

Thus, $\dfrac{b}{s} = \dfrac{2w}{\dfrac{w}{3}} = 2w \bullet \dfrac{3}{w} = \dfrac{6}{1}$.

6) $\dfrac{3}{5}$

Let x= number of adult tickets sold

   3x= number of child tickets sold

Let y= cost of a child ticket

   2y= cost of an adult ticket

Revenue from children's tickets, then, is 3xy (which is the product of the cost of a ticket and the number of tickets sold) and revenue from adults' tickets is 2xy.

Children's tickets are then 3xy out of the total of 5xy (which is the sum of adult revenue and children revenue.) To find the fractional part that children's ticket sale revenue is of total ticket revenue:

$\dfrac{\text{Part}}{\text{Whole}} = \dfrac{3xy}{5xy} = \dfrac{3}{5}$

Alternatively, you can choose values for the cost and number of tickets.

Let children's tickets cost $5. Then adult tickets would cost $10. And let 300 be the number of children's tickets sold. Then 100 adult tickets would be sold.

Therefore, a total of $1,500 would be spent on children's tickets (5 • 300= 1500) and $1,000 would be spent on adult tickets (10 • 100). Thus, $1,500 would be spent on children's tickets out of a total $2,500 spent in all:

$$\frac{1,500}{2,500} = \frac{3}{5}$$

7) **e**

If the waterslide and rollercoaster are 3.5 inches apart on the map, and 1/4 of an inch represents 200 meters, set up the following proportion and cross multiply to find the value of x:

$$\frac{\frac{1}{4}}{200} = \frac{3.5}{x}$$

$$\frac{1}{4}x = 200 • 3.5$$

$$\frac{1}{4}x = 700$$

$$4(\frac{1}{4}x = 700)$$

$$x = 2,800$$

8) **b**

First, since the question asks for minutes, convert 45 seconds to $\frac{3}{4}$ of a minute,

(since $\frac{45}{60} = \frac{3}{4}$).

$$\frac{12 \text{ pages}}{\frac{3}{4} \text{ minutes}} = \frac{90 \text{ pages}}{x \text{ minutes}}$$

$12 \bullet x = \frac{3}{4} \bullet 90$ Cross multiply

$12x = 67.5$ Simplify

$x \quad = 5.625$ Divide both sides by 12

Round 5.625 to 6.

9) **a**

Let x represent the number of pages and y represent the time. We must
 solve for y:

$$\frac{12 \text{ pages}}{\frac{3}{4} \text{ minutes}} = \frac{x \text{ pages}}{y \text{ minutes}}$$

$$12y = \frac{3}{4}x$$

$$\frac{12y}{12} = \frac{\frac{3}{4}}{12}x$$

$$y = \frac{3}{4} \cdot \frac{1}{12}x = \frac{3}{48}x = \frac{1}{16}x$$

Note that $\frac{1}{16}x$ is equivalent to $\frac{x}{16}$.

10) **c**

$$\frac{\frac{2}{3}}{80} = \frac{x}{120}$$

$$\frac{2}{3} \cdot 120 = 80x$$

$$80 = 80x$$

$$x = 1$$

It will take one hour, or 60 minutes.

11) **d**

Since 12 free throws can be made in 2 minutes, set up the following proportion and solve for y:

$$\frac{12}{2} = \frac{x}{y}$$, where y represents the time it takes to shoot x free throws

$$12y = 2x$$

$$y = \frac{x}{6}$$

Chapter 4: Run of the Mill

(Averages and Other Statistical Measures)

4.1 Averages

In order to summarize information about large quantities of data, one might employ the use of averages.

Following are some of the terms associated with averages:

Mean—the sum of all the numbers in the set, divided by the number of numbers in the set:

$$\text{mean} = \frac{\text{sum}}{\text{\# of numbers}}$$

Median—the number in the middle, when the numbers are in order from least to greatest. If there are two middle numbers (which is the case whenever there is an even number of numbers in the set), calculate the mean of those two middle numbers.

Mode—the number listed the most times in a set of numbers

Range—the difference between the highest number and the lowest number in a set

Check-in:

Given the following numbers: 5, 7, 3, 11, 14, 5, find the:

1) Mean
2) Median
3) Mode
4) Range

Solutions:

1) **Mean: 7.5**

$$\frac{5+5+7+3+11+14}{6} = 7.5$$

2) **Median: 6**

To correctly identify the median, first put the numbers in consecutive order: 3, 5, 5, 7, 11, 14. Since there are two numbers in the middle— 5 and 7— take the mean of these two numbers: (5+7)/2= 6 to calculate the median.

3) **Mode: 5**

There are two 5s and one of every other number.

4) **Range: 11**

Highest number minus lowest number: 14 -3 = 11.

Example 4.1

The Banana Cafe sold 30, 70, 92, and 80 pieces of banana cake, Monday through Thursday, respectively. If, on Friday, the Cafe's average for the week (Monday-Friday) was 65 pieces per day, how many pieces of banana cake were sold on Friday?

Solution:

53

In order to have an average of 65 pieces per day, Banana Cafe would have to sell a total of 325 pieces of cake for the week:

$$\frac{\text{sum}}{\text{\# of numbers}} = \text{average}$$

$$\frac{x}{5} = 65$$

In order to solve for x, multiply both sides by 5 to get x=325.

That means that The Cafe sold a total of 325 pieces of cake that week. Subtract from this total the sum of what was sold on Monday through Thursday (30 + 70 + 92 + 80) to find out that 53 pieces were sold on Friday.

Example 4.2

Tommy scored 530 points in seven rounds of his favorite video game. If he scored at least 30 points each round, and earned two of the same score only once, what is the highest possible score he could earn, given that he could only score in 10-point increments (meaning, in multiples of 10)?

Solution:

250

In order for Tommy to score as high as possible, first make his other scores as low as possible. Since Tommy can only earn one score twice, repeat the lowest score:

30   30   40   50   60   70   x

Add up the first six scores and subtract the sum from 530 to find x.

4.2 Weighted Averages

In high school, if you (well, not you, but someone you know) got an F (0 points) in biology and an A (4.0) in gym class, would the GPA balance out to a C (2.0)?

Probably not! Even though the average of 0 and 4 is 2, biology class is likely worth more credits than gym class. If gym class is worth 1 credit and biology is worth 3 credits, for example, the biology class would be worth three times the gym class. The way you would calculate the GPA, then, would be to find the **weighted average**: That is, multiply each input (in this case, the points earned in biology and the points earned in gym) by its weight (3 and 1, respectively), and then divide by the sum of the weights:

$$\frac{0(3)+4(1)}{3+1}=\frac{4}{4}=1$$

This works out to a D average (1.0). Now that's a GPA that would surely have gotten you (I mean, that someone you know) kicked off the football team.

Example 4.3

Leah earned $40,160 a year for 2.5 years and $50,000 a year for the next 3.5 years. What was her average salary over this time period?

a) 45,000
b) 45,080
c) 45,160
d) 45,900
e) 46,100

Solution:

d

This is a weighted average problem, where 2.5 years and 3.5 years serve as the "weights":

$$\frac{40,160 \cdot 2.5 + 50,000 \cdot 3.5}{2.5+3.5} = \frac{100,400+175,000}{6} = 45,900$$

4.3 Standard Deviation

Standard deviation is a measure of the spread of data in a set of numbers, based on every number in the set. Standard deviation measures how far data values are spread out relative to the mean.

To calculate standard deviation (with example):

(Assume data set is : 3, 5, 7, and 9. This set has a mean of 6.)

1) Find the difference between each data point and the mean of the data.

$3 - 6 = -3, \quad 5 - 6 = -1, \quad 7 - 6 = 1, \quad 9 - 6 = 3$

2) Find the sum of the squares of each of these differences:

$(-3)^2 + (-1)^2 + (1)^2 + (3)^2 = 20$

3) Divide the sum by n, the number of numbers in the set:

$$\frac{20}{4} = 5$$

4) Take the square root of the result:

$\sqrt{5}$

Don't expect to be asked to calculate standard deviation. Instead, expect to be given the standard deviation or information about the standard deviation of a set of data, and asked to interpret or make inferences about the data.

Example 4.4

If the mean of the class's test scores was 72, with a standard deviation of 12, how many standard deviations below the mean is a score of 42 points?

Solution:

2.5

A score of 42 points is 30 points below the mean. To find out how many standard deviations below the mean this is, divide 12 into 30, which is 2.5.

In other words, since 30 is 2.5 times 12, the score is 2.5 standard deviations below the mean.

Example 4.5

If the mean of a data set is 12 and the standard deviation is 2, then what is the range of data (from minimum to maximum) at or within two standard deviations of the mean?

Solution:

8 to 16

To find two standard deviations above or below the mean, add or subtract twice the standard deviation from the mean: 12 +/- 2(2).

If data are **normally distributed**, their mean, median, and mode are approximately equal, and the data values are symmetric about the mean, reflecting a "bell" shape.

For normally distributed data, roughly 2/3 of the data fall within 1 standard deviation of the mean, and nearly all the data fall within 2 standard deviations of the mean.

Example 4.6

If a group of 1,900 basketball players are approximately normally distributed with a mean height of 78 inches and standard deviation of 6 inches:

a) Approximately what fractional part of basketball players are between 72 and 84 inches tall?

b) Approximately what fractional part of basketball players are within one standard deviation above the mean?

Solution:

a)

$$\frac{2}{3}$$

If data are normally distributed, approximately $\frac{2}{3}$ of the data fall within one standard deviation of the mean. The range 72 to 84 is a range one standard deviation below and one standard deviation above the mean.

b)

$$\frac{1}{3}$$

If data are normally distributed, approximately $\frac{2}{3}$ of the data fall within one standard deviation of the mean. And, since the data fall along a bell curve, half of that $\frac{2}{3}$s falls above the mean and the other half falls below the mean. Half of $\frac{2}{3}$ is $\frac{1}{3}$.

CHAPTER 4 PRACTICE SET:

1) If Carole spent $22 on 7 knick knacks, and the average of four of the knick knacks was $3.50, what was the approximate average cost of the remaining knick knacks?

a) $2.50

b) $2.67

c) $3.14

d) $3.50

e) $3.62

2) The average temperature was 88 degrees last week and 92 degrees the three days that followed. What was the average temperature over the 10-day period?

a) 88.0

b) 89.2

c) 89.6

d) 90.0

e) 91.2

3) How much money (in dollars) did Elgin gross if he sold three of his paintings for an average of $495 each and two of his paintings for an average of $895 each?

4) What was the average speed of the motorcyclist if he rode for one hour in the city at 40 miles per hour and for four hours on the highway at 80

miles per hour?

a) 56

b) 60

c) 68

d) 72

e) 84

5) What is the mean of the median and mode of the following numbers?:
1, 9, 5, 10, 16, 16, 12

┌─────────────┐
│   │
│   │
└─────────────┘

6) In the following list of positive integers y, 1, 3, x, 6, 8, 9, 8 which of the following could be the average of x and y, where y<x<5, if the data set has modes of 3 and 8?

Indicate all that apply.

a) 2.0

b) 2.5

c) 3.0

d) 3.5

e) 4.0

f) 4.5

g) 5.0

7)
Quantity A	Quantity B
The mean of	The mean of
2, 8, and x	0, 2, 8, and x

8)

Quantity A	Quantity B
The mean of	The mean of
$1, 11,$ and x	$0, 10,$ and $x + 2$

9) What is the mean of $3m + 3$, $6n - 2$, and $6 + 9p$?

a) $m + n + p + \dfrac{7}{3}$

b) $m + 2n + 3p + \dfrac{7}{3}$

c) $m - 2n + 3p + \dfrac{7}{3}$

d) $m + 2n + 3p + 7$

e) $3m + 6n + 9p + 7$

10) Shawn drove x miles at 40 miles per hour and y miles at 60 miles per hour. What was his average speed?

a) $\dfrac{xy(x + y)}{100}$

b) $\dfrac{40y + 60x}{(xy)(x + y)}$

c) $\dfrac{(xy)(x + y)}{40y + 60x}$

d) $\dfrac{120(x + y)}{3x + 2y}$

e) $\dfrac{3x + 2y}{120(x + y)}$

11) If Stephen scored between 1 and 2 standard deviations (inclusive) below the class average of 58, what score could he have earned, given a standard deviation of 6?

Indicate <u>all</u> that apply.

a) 45
b) 48
c) 52
d) 54
e) 56

SOLUTIONS: Chapter 4 Practice Set

1) b
2) b
3) 3,275
4) d
5) 13
6) b and d
7) d
8) c
9) b
10) d
11) b and c

EXPLANATIONS: Chapter 4 Practice Set

1) **b**

If the average of 4 of the knick knacks was $3.50, then the total spent on the 4 knick knacks was $14, found by manipulating the average formula: average= sum/#.

$$3.50 = \frac{sum}{4}$$ Multiply both sides by 4

$$14.00 = sum$$

That leaves $8 left of the $22 she spent. The average of the remaining knick knacks, then, was:

$$\frac{\text{sum}}{\#} = \frac{8}{3} = 2.67 \text{ (rounded)}.$$

2) **b**

This is a weighted average question:

$$\frac{(88 \bullet 7) + (92 \bullet 3)}{(7 + 3)} = 89.2$$

3) **3,275**

$$\text{average} = \frac{\text{sum}}{\#}$$

$$495 = \frac{\text{sum}_1}{3} \rightarrow \text{sum}_1 = 495 \bullet 3 = 1,485$$

$$895 = \frac{\text{sum}_2}{2} \rightarrow \text{sum}_2 = 895 \bullet 2 = 1,790$$

Elgin grossed a total of $3,275 (1,485 + 1,790).

4) **d**

Weighted average:

$$\frac{40 \bullet 1 + 80 \bullet 4}{(1 + 4)} = 72$$

5) **13**

First, put the numbers in ascending order: 1, 5, 9, 10, 12, 16, 16

Median: 10

Mode: 16

Mean of Median and Mode:

$$\frac{10+16}{2}=13$$

6) **b and d**

Since both 3 and 8 are modes, and there are two 8s, then there must be two 3s. One of the missing values, then, must be 3. Since x>y, if x is 3 then y must be 2. (Note that y cannot be 1, because that would make 1 an additional mode.) If y is 3, then x must be 4 (since y<x<5). Once you figure out what x and y can be, add them and divide by 2 to get the possible averages.

7) **d**

Both columns add to the same value, which is 10 + x. To find the average of Column A, divide the sum by 3, and to find the average of Column B, divide the sum by 4. If the numerator is positive (meaning x>-10), dividing by 3 will result in a larger quotient than dividing by 4. If the numerator is negative (meaning, x<-10), dividing by 4 will result in a larger quotient than dividing by 3.

8) **c**

Again, both columns add to the same value, which is 12 + x. But in this case, both sums are divided by 3. So the results are equal.

9) **b**

Add the terms together and then divide by 3:

$$\frac{3m+3+6n-2+6+9p}{3} = \frac{3m+6n+9p+7}{3} = m+2n+3p+\frac{7}{3}$$

10) **d**

total distance = x + y

$$\text{total time} = \frac{x}{40} + \frac{y}{60}$$

$$\text{average speed} = \frac{\text{total distance}}{\text{total time}}$$

$$\frac{x+y}{\dfrac{x}{40}+\dfrac{y}{60}}$$

$$\frac{x+y}{\dfrac{3x}{120}+\dfrac{2y}{120}}$$ Get a common denominator for the fractions in the denominator.

113

$$\frac{\dfrac{x+y}{3x+2y}}{120}$$ Add the fractions in the denominator.

$$\frac{x+y}{1} \bullet \frac{120}{3x+2y}$$ Multiply by the reciprocal of the denominator.

$$\frac{120(x+y)}{3x+2y}$$ Multiply the fractions.

.

11) **b and c**

If Stephen earned a score that was 1 to 2 standard deviations below the mean, he had to score between 58-2(6)= 46 [which is 2 standard deviations below the mean] and 58 - 6=52 [which is 1 standard deviation below the mean].

Chapter 5: Express Yourself!

(Expressions)

5.1 Expressions

Expressions are comprised of any combination of numbers, variables, and/or operations. Examples include: $3 \cdot 2 - 6$, $2x + 7$ and $3(5y+2)$. When given an expression with a variable, if you are given a value for that variable, you can evaluate the expression by substituting the given value for the variable.

Example 5.1

a) Find the value of $2x^2 - x - 12$ when $x=12$.

b) Find the value of $-x^5 - x^2$ when $x = 3$.

Solution:

a) **264**

$2(12)^2 - 12 - 12 = 288 - 12 - 12 = 264$

b) **-252**

$-3^5 - 3^2 = -243 - 9 = -252$

It is also useful to simplify expressions that cannot be evaluated.

5.2 Combining Like Terms

We can simplify expressions by combining **like terms** [terms that have the same combination of variable(s) raised to the same respective power(s)]

115

through addition and subtraction. Below are a few examples of like terms:

1) $4x$ and $2x$ 2) $5x^5$ and $9x^5$ 3) $3x^2y^3z$ and $-7x^2y^3z$

Check-in:

Simplify the following expressions (by combining like terms):

a) $2x + 9x + 4$ b) $8x^2 + 5x - 12$ c) $4x^2y - 3xy^2$

d) $4m + 7 - 8m$ e) $4y - 8 + 2y - 9$ f) $2z^2 + 4z - 8z^2$

Solution:

a) $11x + 4$ b) already simplified   c) already simplified

d) $-4m + 7$ e) $6y - 17$ f) $-6z^2 + 4z$

5.3 Multiplying Expressions

In order to multiply two **binomials** (expressions comprised of the sum or difference of two terms), perform an extension of the distributive property, where each term in the first binomial is multiplied by each term in the second binomial.

Use the acronym **FOIL— which stands for First, Outside, Inside, Last—** to guide you by telling you which numbers you need to multiply:

For example: (a+b) • (c+d)

First   Outside   Inside   Last
$a \cdot c$ + $a \cdot d$ + $b \cdot c$ + $b \cdot d$

Check-in:

Find the product of (x+3) and (x+7)

Solution:

$$x^2 + 10x + 21$$

The product of (x+3) and (x+7) can be written as: (x+3)(x+7).

Then, use FOIL to multiply:

First	Outside	Inside	Last
$x \bullet x$ +	$7 \bullet x$ +	$3 \bullet x$ +	$3 \bullet 7$

$x^2 + 7x + 3x + 21$

$x^2 + 10x + 21$

Check-in:

Multiply the following binomials:

a) $(z+9)(z+2)$ b) $(y+6)(y+11)$
c) $(x-7)(x+2)$ d) $(x+1)(x-1)$
e) $(2m+8)(3m+5)$ f) $(2v-20)(v-2)$

Solution:

a) $z^2 + 11z + 18$ b) $y^2 + 17y + 66$
c) $x^2 - 5x - 14$ d) $x^2 - 1$
e) $6m^2 + 34m + 40$ f) $2v^2 - 24v + 40$

5.4 Factoring Expressions:

Much like factoring numbers, when factoring an expression, you are looking to find two or more factors that multiply together to get your original expression.

Following are various methods of factoring **polynomials,** which are expressions comprised of the sum or difference of two or more terms.

Factor out the Greatest Common Factor:

In the expression $3x + 9$, you'll notice that each term is divisible by 3. Therefore, you can factor out a 3 and re-write the expression as: $3(x+3)$.

Notice that this is the reverse order of the distributive property.
Instead of multiplying each term by 3, you are dividing each term by 3. That which you are dividing by is placed on the outside of the parentheses to maintain the value of the expression. Try a few.

Check-in:

a) $25x^2 + 5x - 15$ b) $6x + 12xy + 22x^2y$

c) $-5a + 10b + 15c$ d) $49m^2n^3 + 343mn^2$

Solution:

a) $5(5x^2 + x - 3)$ b) $2x(3 + 6y + 11xy)$

c) $5(-a + 2b + 3c)$ or $-5(a - 2b - 3c)$ d) $49mn^2(mn + 7)$

Factoring Polynomials:

After you have factored out the greatest common factor (when possible), you can **do the reverse of FOIL to further factor (break down) your polynomial:**

The most common polynomials to factor are of the form $x^2 + bx + c$.

$x^2 + bx + c = (x+e)(x+f)$, where $c = e \cdot f$ and $b = e+f$. That is, you need two numbers that:

1) multiply together to give you c, and
2) add together to give you b.

Take $x^2 + 6x + 8$. In order to factor this polynomial, you need two numbers that multiply together to give you 8 and add together to give you 6. Those two numbers are 4 and 2:

$$x^2 + 6x + 8 = (x+2)(x+4)$$

Common Quadratic Forms:

The following squared expressions are called **quadratics**, because they are expressions raised to the second power.

$$(a+b)^2 = a^2 + 2ab + b^2$$
$$(a-b)^2 = a^2 - 2ab + b^2$$
$$(a-b)(a+b) = a^2 - b^2$$

Memorizing how the factored form (left) turns into the unfactored form (right) and vice versa will save you time on test day.

Check-in:

Factor the following polynomials:

a) $y^2 + 11y + 18$ b) $x^2 + 16x + 64$

c) $x^2 + 9x + 14$ d) $x^2 + 2x + 1$

e) $m^2 + 13m + 40$ f) $m^2 + 22m + 40$

g) $x^2 - 9x + 18$ h) $x^2 - 3x - 18$

i) $x^2 - 25$ j) $4x^2 - 9y^2$

k) $x^2 - 9$ l) $49x^2 - 36$

m) $2x^2 - 50$ n) $16x^4 - 1$

Solution:

a) $(y + 9)(y + 2)$ b) $(x + 8)(x + 8)$ or $(x + 8)^2$

c) $(x + 7)(x + 2)$ d) $(x + 1)(x + 1)$ or $(x + 1)^2$

e) $(m + 8)(m + 5)$ f) $(m + 20)(m + 2)$

g) $(x - 3)(x - 6)$ h) $(x - 6)(x + 3)$

i) $(x - 5)(x + 5)$ j) $(2x - 3y)(2x + 3y)$

k) $(x - 3)(x + 3)$ l) $(7x - 6)(7x + 6)$

m) $2(x - 5)(x + 5)$ n) $(4x^2 + 1)(2x - 1)(2x + 1)$

Note that for n), once you factor $16x^4 - 1 = (4x^2 + 1)(4x^2 - 1)$, the second term can be further factored into $(2x-1)(2x+1)$.

Example 5.1

What is the greatest common factor of:
$x^2 - 5x - 14$; $x^2 - 7x$; and $2x^2 - 11x - 21$?

a) x-3

b) x+3

c) x -7

d) x +7

e) x-21

120

Solution:

c) x-7

Factor each polynomial:

$$x^2 - 5x - 14 \quad = (x-7)(x+2)$$

$$x^2 - 7x \quad\quad = x(x-7)$$

$$2x^2 - 11x - 21 = (2x+3)(x-7)$$

Each polynomial has a factor of $(x-7)$.

Example 5.2

Evaluate the following expression for $x = \dfrac{2}{3}$:

$$\frac{x^2 + 3x - 10}{x^2 - 4x} \bullet \frac{x^2 - 6x + 8}{(x-2)^2}$$

Solution:

$$\frac{17}{2}$$

$$\frac{x^2 + 3x - 10}{x^2 - 4x} \bullet \frac{x^2 - 6x + 8}{(x-2)^2}$$

$$\frac{(x+5)(x-2)}{x(x-4)} \bullet \frac{(x-4)(x-2)}{(x-2)(x-2)}$$

$$\frac{(x+5)}{x}$$

Since x=2/3:

$$\frac{(\frac{2}{3}+5)}{\frac{2}{3}} = \frac{\frac{17}{3}}{\frac{2}{3}} = \frac{17}{3} \bullet \frac{3}{2} = \frac{17}{2}$$

CHAPTER 5 PRACTICE SET:

1) If $x^2y = y^2x$ and $x>y$, which of the following could be true?
Indicate <u>all</u> that apply.

a) $x = 0$
b) $y = 0$
c) $x > 0$ and $y > 0$
d) $x = -y$
e) $x > 0$ and $y < 0$

2) Simplify the following expression:

$$\frac{x^3 - 3x^2 + 2x}{x^2 - 4}$$

a) $\dfrac{x - 1}{x + 2}$

b) $\dfrac{x(x - 1)}{x + 2}$

c) $\dfrac{2(x - 1)}{x + 2}$

d) $\dfrac{x + 2}{x - 1}$

e) $\dfrac{x(x + 1)}{x - 2}$

3) What is the value of $(\frac{1}{x} + x)^2$ if $x^2 = 7$?

Write answer as a fraction:

4) What is the value of $3x^{-4}$, if $4x^2 = 12$?

Write answer as a fraction:

5) $x > 0$

Quantity A	Quantity B
$(x+3)^3$	$(x+4)(x+3)(x+2)$

SOLUTIONS: Chapter 5 Practice Set

1) **a and b only**
2) **b**
3) $\dfrac{64}{7}$
4) $\dfrac{1}{3}$
5) **a**

EXPLANATIONS: Chapter 5 Practice Set

1)a and b only

Consider each option in turn:

a) x=0: If x=0, both sides are zero.

b)y=0: If y=0, both sides are zero.

c)x>0 and y>0:

Solve for x in terms of y:

$$x^2 y = y^2 x$$

$$xy = y^2$$

$$x = y$$

This is not possible because x>y, per the given information.

d) x= -y: Since we know that x>y, if x did equal the opposite of y, we know that x would be positive and y would be negative. This would make the left side of the equation negative, and the right side of the equation positive, so the relationship does not hold.

e) x>0 and y<0: As in answer choice d, the left side of the equation would be negative and the right side would be positive.

2) **b**

$$\frac{x^3 - 3x^2 + 2x}{x^2 - 4}$$

$$\frac{x(x^2 - 3x + 2)}{x^2 - 4}$$

$$\frac{x(x-1)(x-2)}{(x+2)(x-2)}$$

$$\frac{x(x-1)}{(x+2)}$$

3) $\dfrac{\textbf{64}}{\textbf{7}}$

$$(\frac{1}{x} + x)^2$$

$(\frac{1}{x} + x)(\frac{1}{x} + x)$ FOIL the numbers

$$(\frac{1}{x})^2 + (\frac{1}{x})x + (\frac{1}{x})x + x^2$$

$\dfrac{1}{x^2} + 1 + 1 + x^2$ The product of a number and its reciprocal is 1.

$$\frac{1}{x^2} + 2 + x^2$$

Since $x^2 = 7$:

$$(\frac{1}{7} + 2 + 7)$$

$$9\frac{1}{7} \text{ or } \frac{64}{7}$$

Note that it was not necessary to solve for x, as the expression simplified to x^2 terms and we are given $x^2=7$.

4) $\dfrac{1}{3}$

Since $4x^2 = 12$, $x^2 = 3$.

Re-write $3x^{-4}$ as: $\dfrac{3}{x^4} = \dfrac{3}{(x^2)^2} = \dfrac{3}{(3)^2} = \dfrac{3}{9} = \dfrac{1}{3}$.

5) **a**

Quantity A	Quantity B
$(x+3)^3$	$(x+4)(x+3)(x+2)$
$(x+3)(x+3)(x+3)$	$(x+4)(x+3)(x+2)$
$(x+3)(x+3)$	$(x+4)(x+2)$
$x^2 + 6x + 9$	$x^2 + 6x + 8$
9	8

Chapter 6: Balance Beam

(Equations and Inequalities)

6.1 Equations

An equation is formed by setting two equivalent expressions equal (=) to each other. The expressions can be as simple as a lone number (called a **constant,** because its value does not change). An example of such an equation is:

$$2x+7 =15$$

To solve an equation, your goal is to find the value(s) of a variable that make the equation true. This is done by **isolating** the variable (meaning, getting the variable by itself on one side of an equation). The simplest way to do this is to follow the REVERSE of the order of operations, combining like terms whenever possible along the way. That is, flip **PEMDAS** (You still remember Please Excuse My Dear Aunt Sally from Chapter 1, don't you?) and make it **SADMEP** (How about, "Sassy And Dainty Molly Eats Polenta?" No? Don't like? Hmmph. Well, come up with your own then!)

Use **SADMEP** to help you solve the following equations, where your goal is to solve the equation by isolating the variable. **In order to isolate a variable, you are required to "undo" that which is being done to your variable while following SADMEP.**

For example, if there is a term added to the variable that you wish to isolate, subtract that number. And if there is a number multiplied to the variable that you wish to isolate, divide by that number.

To solve the equation from the chapter's opening:

$$2x + 7 = 15$$ Undo adding 7 by subtracting 7 from both sides.

$$\underline{\quad -7 \quad -7 \quad}$$

$$2x \quad = 8$$

$$\frac{2x}{2} = \frac{8}{2}$$ Undo multiplying by 2 by dividing both sides by 2.

$$x = 4$$

Check-in:

a) $3x + 7 = 22$ b) $2x^2 + 6 = 24$ c) $5x + 8x - 7 = 12$

d) $\sqrt{x} + 9 = 21$ e) $(\frac{2}{3})x - (\frac{1}{5})x = 14$

f) $\frac{x}{9} + 7 = 12$ g) $3(x + 7) - 8 = -9$

Solution:

a) **x = 5**

$$3x + 7 = 22$$

$$\underline{\quad -7 \quad -7 \quad}$$

$$3x \quad = 15$$

$$\frac{3x}{3} = \frac{15}{3}$$

$$x \quad = 5$$

b) **x = +/- 3**

$$2x^2 + 6 = 24$$
$$\underline{\quad - 6 \quad - 6}$$
$$2x^2 \quad = 18$$

$$\frac{2x^2}{2} = \frac{18}{2}$$

$$x^2 \quad = \quad 9$$

$$\sqrt{x^2} \quad = +/- \sqrt{9}$$

$$x \quad = +/- 3$$

Note: When you take the square root of a squared variable, there are two answers: the positive answer and the negative answer (unless the answer is zero). That's because the original value of the variable can be positive or negative:

$$(-3)^2 = 9 \quad \text{and} \quad (3)^2 = 9$$

c) **x = $\frac{19}{13}$**

$$5x + 8x - 7 = 12$$
$$13x \quad - 7 = 12$$
$$\underline{\quad\quad + 7 \quad + 7}$$
$$13x \quad\quad = 19$$

$$\frac{13x}{13} = \frac{19}{13}$$

$$x \quad\quad = \frac{19}{13}$$

d) **x = 144**

$$\sqrt{x} + 9 = 21$$
$$\underline{\quad -9 \quad -9 \quad}$$
$$\sqrt{x} \quad = 12$$

$$(\sqrt{x})^2 = (12)^2$$

$$x \quad = 144$$

e) **x=30**

$$\frac{2}{3}x - \frac{1}{5}x = 14$$

$$\frac{10}{15}x - \frac{3}{15}x = 14$$

$$\frac{7}{15}x \quad = 14$$

$$\frac{15}{7}\left(\frac{7}{15}x \quad = 14\right)$$

$$x \quad = 14 \cdot \frac{15}{7} = 30$$

f) **x=45**

$$\frac{x}{9} + 7 = 12$$

$$\underline{\quad -7 \quad -7 \quad}$$

$$\frac{x}{9} = 5$$

$$9\left(\frac{x}{9} = 5\right)$$

$$x = 45$$

g) $\mathbf{x = -\dfrac{22}{3}}$

$$3(x + 7) - 8 = -9$$

$$3x + 21 - 8 = -9$$

$$3x + 13 = -9$$

$$\underline{\quad -13 \qquad -13 \quad}$$

$$3x = -22$$

$$\frac{3x}{3} = \frac{-22}{3}$$

$$x = \frac{-22}{3}$$

6. 2 Simultaneous Equations:

Sometimes you will be given two or more equations with at least two variables and asked to solve for one or more of the variables or asked to find the average of the variables.

Years ago in algebra class when you were tasked with solving simultaneous equations, you learned several different methods of solving them. On the

GRE, however, you are often asked questions in such a way that by adding or subtracting one equation from the other, one variable cancels out.

Example 6.1

Find the value of x and y that satisfies the following system of equations:

$2x + 7y = 12$ and $5x - 7y = 9$.

Solution:

$$x = 3 \text{ and } y = \frac{6}{7}$$

Note that the first equation adds 7y and the second subtracts 7y. Since these two terms have opposite signs, they are inverse terms. To cancel the y terms, we simply add the two equations together:

$$
\begin{array}{r}
2x + 7y = 12 \\
+5x - 7y = 9 \\
\hline
7x = 21
\end{array}
$$

$$\frac{7x}{7} = \frac{21}{7}$$

$$x = 3$$

Then, substitute 3 for x into either of the original equations to solve for y. Let's say we take the first equation:

$$2x \quad + 7y = 12$$
$$2(3) + 7y = 12$$
$$6 \quad + 7y = 12$$

$$\underline{-6 \qquad\qquad -6}$$

$$7y = 6$$

$$\frac{7y}{7} = \frac{6}{7}$$

$$y = \frac{6}{7}$$

Example 6.2 Based on the following system of equations, what is the average of x, y, and z?

$$2x + 3y \qquad = 12$$
$$5x + 8y - z \quad = 15$$
$$4x \qquad + 12z = 9$$

Solution:

$$\frac{12}{11}$$

Note that you are being asked to find the average of the variables. It is inconsequential what the values of the individual variables are—you only need to know the sum of these variables in order to calculate the average.

This example is similar to the previous example. To solve, just add your equations together, combining like terms:

$$2x + 3y \quad = 12$$
$$5x + 8y - z \quad = 15$$
$$\underline{4x \quad + 12z = \quad 9}$$
$$11x + 11y + 11z = 36$$

(Conveniently, all the coefficients are the same. This is common on a GRE problem like this.)

$$11(x + y + z) = 36$$

$$\frac{11(x + y + z)}{11} = \frac{36}{11}$$

$$x + y + z \quad = \frac{36}{11}$$

Now, to find the average, divide the sum by 3.

$$\frac{x + y + z}{3} = \frac{\frac{36}{11}}{3}$$

$$\frac{x + y + z}{3} = \frac{36}{11} \bullet \frac{1}{3} = \frac{36}{33} = \frac{12}{11}$$

Zero Product Property:

From Chapter 1, the **Zero Product Property** indicates that the product of two or more numbers is zero if one or more of the factors is zero: $x \bullet 0 = 0$.

This property helps us solve some quadratic equations.

Example 6.3

If $3x^2 + 30x + 60 = -15$, what is the value of $x+8$?

Solution:

3

First, set the equation equal to zero.

$$\begin{array}{rcl} 3x^2 + 30x + 60 & = & -15 \\ +15 & & +15 \\ \hline 3x^2 + 30x + 75 & = & 0 \end{array}$$

Factor out the greatest common factor:

$3(x^2 + 10x + 25) = 0$

Divide both sides by 3:

$$\frac{3(x^2 + 10x + 25)}{3} = \frac{0}{3}$$

$$x^2 + 10x + 25 = 0$$

Factor the polynomial and set each term equal to zero and solve. (Since the factored terms are the same in this case, set one of them equal to zero.)

$(x+5)(x+5) = 0$

$$\begin{array}{rcl} x+5 & = & 0 \\ -5 & & -5 \\ \hline x & = & -5 \end{array}$$

Since $x = -5$, $x + 8 = 3$.

Note: To solve a problem on the GRE, when you are given a factored polynomial you often need to unfactor it, and when given an unfactored polynomial, you often need to factor it.

Example 6.4

If $x^2 + y^2 = 9$ and $(x+y)^2 + 12 = 33$, what is the value of $5xy$?

Solution:

30

There are three things that you should note in order to solve this problem:

1) $x^2 + y^2$ cannot be factored, so we cannot use the first equation yet
2) $(x+y)^2$ can be unfactored: $(x+y)^2 = (x+y)(x+y) = x^2 + 2xy + y^2$
3) Only the product of x and y is being asked for—so we do not need to solve for x or y individually

$$
\begin{array}{lll}
(x+y)^2 + 12 & = 33 & \text{Expand } (x+y)^2 \\
(x+y)(x+y) + 12 & = 33 & \\
x^2 + 2xy + y^2 + 12 & = 33 & \text{FOIL} \\
\quad\quad\quad\quad -12 \quad -12 & & \\
\hline
x^2 + 2xy + y^2 & = 21 &
\end{array}
$$

$$x^2 + y^2 + 2xy \quad = 21 \qquad \text{Re-arrange the terms}$$

$$9 + 2xy \quad = 21 \qquad \text{Substitute 9 in for } x^2 + y^2$$

$$
\begin{array}{rr}
9 + 2xy & = 21 \\
-9 & -9 \\
\hline
2xy & = 12 \\
\end{array}
$$

$$\frac{2xy}{2} = \frac{12}{2}$$

$$xy = 6$$

And finally, don't forget to answer the question : What is 5xy?
Since xy = 6, 5xy = 30.

Example 6.5

If $x^2 + 6x + 9 = 36$, what could be the value of $x + 3$?

a)-9

b)-6

c)-3

d)0

e)3

f)6

Solution:

b, f

$x^2 + 6x + 9 = 36$ Set the equation equal to zero by subtracting 36

$$\frac{-36}{x^2 + 6x - 27} = \frac{-36}{0}$$ from both sides of the equation.

$(x - 3)(x + 9) = 0$

$x = 3$ or -9

Thus, $x + 3 = 6$ or -6.

Example 6.6

If $x^2 + 12x + 32 = 0$, what is the sum of the solutions of the equation?

Solution:

-12

Factor the polynomial. By the Zero Product Property, at least one of the factors is zero. Therefore, set each factor equal to zero. The solution to these equations will tell you the values of x that make the equation true.

$x^2 + 12x + 32 = 0$
$(x + 8)(x + 4) = 0$ Factor the polynomial.

$x + 8 = 0$ or $x + 4 = 0$ Set each factor equal to zero and solve each equation.
$\dfrac{-8\ -8}{x = -8}$ $\dfrac{-4\ -4}{x = -4}$

The sum of the solutions, then, is -12: -8+-4= -12.

Quadratic Formula

Some polynomials are difficult to factor, making the equations that contain them difficult to solve. When the polynomial is part of a **quadratic equation** use **the quadratic formula**. That is, for any equation written in the form of: $ax^2+bx+c = 0$, such that $a \neq 0$, you can solve for x using the following formula:

$$x = \frac{-b \pm \sqrt{b^2 - 4ac}}{2a}$$

Example 6.7

What is the product of the solutions of the following equation?:
$3x^2 + 10x - 47 = 10$.

Solution:

-19

First, set the equation equal to zero by subtracting 10 from both sides:
$3x^2 + 10x - 57 = 0$.

Then, use the quadratic formula:

$$x = \frac{-b \pm \sqrt{b^2 - 4ac}}{2a}$$, where a = 3, b= 10, and c= -57

$$x = \frac{-10 \pm \sqrt{10^2 - 4 \cdot 3 \cdot -57}}{2 \cdot 3}$$

$$x = \frac{-10 \pm \sqrt{100 + 684}}{6}$$

$$x = \frac{-10 \pm 28}{6}$$

$$x = \frac{-10 + 28}{6} \text{ or } x = \frac{-10 - 28}{6}$$

$$x = 3 \text{ or } \frac{-19}{3}$$

The product of the solutions of x, then, is -19: $3 \cdot \frac{-19}{3} = -19$.

6.3 Inequalities

Inequalities are solved in the same way that equations are solved, with one exception: When you multiply or divide by a negative number, the direction of the inequality sign reverses.

Check-in:

Solve the following inequalities:

a) $3x + 12 > 15$ b) $-2x + 4 \leq 12$

Solution:

a) **x > 1**   b) **x ≥ -4**

141

a) $3x + 12 > 15$

$$\underline{ -12 \;\; -12}$$

$3x > 3$

$x > 1$

b) $-2x + 4 \geq 12$

$$\underline{ -4 \;\; -4}$$

$-2x \geq 8$

$x \leq -4$ (Note new sign direction, because we divided by a negative.)

For inequalities involving absolute values:

$|x + c| < d$ means: $-d < x + c < d$

$|x + c| > d$ means: $x + c > d$ or $x + c < -d$

Check-in:

a) Solve: $|x + 12| < 8$

b) Solve: $|2x + 10| > 12$

Solution:

a) **-20 < x < -4**

$|x + 12| < 8 \rightarrow -8 < x + 12 < 8$

$-8 < x + 12 < 8$ Subtract 12 from each side of the inequality.

$$\underline{-12 -12 \; -12}$$

$-20 < x < -4$

b) **x > 1 or x < -11**

$|2x + 10| > 12 \rightarrow 2x + 10 > 12$ or $2x + 10 < -12$

$$2x + 10 > 12 \text{ or } 2x + 10 < -12$$
$$\underline{-10 \quad -10 \qquad \quad -10 \quad -10}$$
$$2x > 2 \qquad \qquad 2x < -22$$

$\dfrac{2x}{2} > \dfrac{2}{2}$ or $\dfrac{2x}{2} < \dfrac{-22}{2}$

$x > 1$ or $x < -11$

CHAPTER 6 PRACTICE SET:

1) Based on the following system of equations, what is the average of a and b, in terms of c?

$3a + 2c = -b$

$a + 3b = c$

a) $\dfrac{-c}{8}$

b) $\dfrac{-c}{4}$

c) $\dfrac{-c}{2}$

d) $\dfrac{c}{4}$

e) $\dfrac{c}{2}$

2) John bought 2 pomegranates and 4 mangoes for a total of $12.00. Christina bought 5 mangoes and 4 apples for a total of $11.50. If pomegranates cost twice as much as mangoes, what was the cost of one apple?

a) 1.00

b) 2.00

c) 2.75

d) 3.50

e) 4.00

3) If $x^2-7x=-12$, what could the value of x^2 be?

Indicate <u>all</u> values that apply.

a)-4

b)-3

c)0

d)3

e) 4

f) 9

g) 16

4) If $|x+12|=37$, what is the average of the possible values of x?

5) If $(x+3)(2x-8)(x^2-9)=0$, what is the product of the distinct solutions of this equation?

6) If $x^2 + 8y = 14$ and $x + 4y = 3$, what is the greatest possible value of x?

7) What is the average of the solutions of the following equation?:

$10x^2 - 29x + 21 = 0$

a) $\dfrac{21}{10}$

b) $\dfrac{29}{20}$

c) $\dfrac{7}{5}$

d) $\dfrac{3}{2}$

e) $\dfrac{29}{10}$

SOLUTIONS: Chapter 6 Practice Set

1) a
2) a
3) f and g
4) -12
5) -36
6) 4
7) b

EXPLANATIONS: Chapter 6 Practice Set

1) **a**

$3a + 2c = -b$

$a + 3b = c$

$3a + 2c = -b$

$\underline{\quad -2c \quad -2c}$

$3a \qquad = -b - 2c$

$\underline{\quad +b \quad +b}$

$3a + b = \qquad -2c$

Manipulate the first equation so that a and b are on the left side and the c term is on the other.

$3a + b = -2c$

$\underline{a + 3b = c}$

$4a + 4b = -c$

Add the manipulated first equation to the second equation.

$4a + 4b = -c$

$4(a + b) = -c$

Factor out the greatest common factor

$\dfrac{4(a + b)}{4} = \dfrac{-c}{4}$

$a + b = \dfrac{-c}{4}$

$\dfrac{(a + b)}{2} = \dfrac{\frac{-c}{4}}{2} = \dfrac{-c}{8}$

Find the average by dividing both sides by 2.

2) **a**

Let P stand for the cost of pomegranates, M for the cost of mangoes, and A for the cost of apples. Then the resulting equations are:

$2P + 4M = 12.00$ (Total cost of John's purchases)

$5M + 4A = 11.50$ (Total cost of Christina's purchases)

$P = 2M$ (A pomegranate costs twice as much as a mango.)

The goal is to solve for A in the second equation. First, find a value for M by using the first equation :

$2P + 4M = 12.00$

$2(2M) + 4M = 12.00$ Substitute 2M for P

$4M + 4M = 12.00$

$8M = 12.00$

$$\frac{8M}{8} = \frac{12.00}{8}$$

$M = 1.50$

Next, substitute $1.50 for M in the second equation and solve for A:

$5M + 4A = 11.50$

$5(1.50) + 4A = 11.50$

$$\begin{array}{r} 7.50 \quad +4A = 11.50 \\ \underline{-7.50 \qquad\qquad -7.50} \\ 0 + 4A \qquad 4.00 \end{array}$$

$$\frac{4A}{4} = \frac{4.00}{4}$$

$$A = 1.00$$

3) **f and g**

$x^2 - 7x \quad = -12$ Set the equation equal to zero.

$$\begin{array}{r} \underline{+12 \qquad +12} \\ x^2 - 7x + 12 = 0 \end{array}$$

$(x - 3)(x - 4) = 0$ Factor the left side of the equation.

$x - 3 = 0$ or $x - 4 = 0$ Set each factor equal to zero and solve.

$$\begin{array}{cc} \underline{+3 \ +3} & \underline{+4 \ +4} \\ x = 3 & x = 4 \end{array}$$

$x^2 = 9$ or $x^2 = 16$ Square each equation.

4) **-12**

If $|x + 12| = 37$, then :

$x + 12 = 37$ or $x + 12 = -37$ Solve the two equations for x.

$$\begin{array}{cc} x + 12 = 37 & \text{or} \quad x + 12 = -37 \\ \underline{-12 \ -12} & \underline{-12 \ -12} \\ x \ = 25 & x = -49 \end{array}$$

$$\frac{25 + \text{-}49}{2} = \frac{\text{-}24}{2} = \text{-}12$$

5) **-36**

Since $(x+3)(2x-8)(x^2-9)=0$, by the Zero Product Property :

$x+3=0$ or $2x-8=0$ or $x^2-9=0$

    $\underline{\text{-}3 \quad \text{-}3}$ $\underline{+8 \quad +8}$ $\underline{+9 \quad +9}$

    $x \quad = \text{-}3$ $2x = 8$ $x^2 = 9$

                    $x=4$ $x = +/\text{-}3$

Product of the distinct (meaning, different) solutions: $\text{-}3 \bullet 4 \bullet 3 = \text{-}36$. Since distinct means different, we don't count -3 twice.

6) **4**

First, double the second equation to: 2x+8y=6, so that there is an "8y" term in each equation. Then, subtract this manipulated second equation from the first equation:

$$x^2 \quad +8y = 14$$
$$\underline{-(\ 2x+8y=6)}$$
$$x^2 - 2x = 8$$

$x^2 - 2x \quad = 8$ Set equal to zero.

      $\underline{-8 \qquad -8}$

$x^2 - 2x - 8 = 0$

$(x-4)(x+2)=0$

$x=4$ or $x=\text{-}2$

The greatest possible value of x, then, is 4.

7) **b**

$10x^2 - 29x + 21 = 0$

$a = 10, b = -29, c = 21$

$$x = \frac{-b \pm \sqrt{b^2 - 4ac}}{2a}$$

$$x = \frac{-(-29) \pm \sqrt{(-29)^2 - 4 \bullet 10 \bullet 21}}{2 \bullet 10}$$

$$x = \frac{29 \pm \sqrt{841 - 840}}{2 \bullet 10}$$

$$x = \frac{29 + 1}{20} \qquad x = \frac{29 - 1}{20}$$

$$x = \frac{3}{2} \qquad x = \frac{7}{5}$$

The average, then, is $\dfrac{\frac{3}{2} + \frac{7}{5}}{2} = \dfrac{\frac{15}{10} + \frac{14}{10}}{2} = \dfrac{\frac{29}{10}}{2} = \dfrac{29}{10} \bullet \dfrac{1}{2} = \dfrac{29}{20}$.

Chapter 7: I Thought This Was MATH, Not English!

(Word Problems)

Word problems are often the bane of a GRE student's existence— but they don't have to be. By becoming familiar with:

1) key words that help you translate problems into equations, and

2) common types of word problems, you will be able to (almost kinda sorta) embrace word problems.

Tool #1: Learn how to translate English into Math.

Math is a language that says in symbols what English says in words. For every key word, there is a mathematical symbol or operation associated with that word. Here are some of the main ones:

> **of:** multiply
>
> **what:** variable
>
> **percent:** multiply by 1/100 or .01
>
> **is:** equals

Example 7.1

Delilah loves scarves, but she decides she needs to pare down her wardrobe. If she donates 80 percent of her scarves, leaving her with just 30 scarves, how many did she give away?

Solution:

120

One way to solve this word problem is to translate the key words into mathematical symbols. But first, you have to think about how the percent given (80%) correlates to the quantity given (30). The 30 remaining scarves represent what's left after Delilah gives away 80% of her collection. Therefore, 30 scarves represents the remaining 20% of her collection. The unknown can be represented by x, the original number of scarves.

20% of her scarves is 30 scarves. Translation: $20\% \cdot x = 30$.

$$20\% \cdot x = 30$$
$$.2x = 30$$

$$\frac{.2x}{.2} = \frac{30}{.2}$$

$$x = 150$$

So, Delilah had 150 scarves. If she has 30 left, she gave 120 away.

Example 7.2

Gina spent one fifth of her paycheck on her Caribbean vacation. She spent half of her remaining paycheck on her favorite charity. If Gina had $225 left, how much money did she donate to her charity?

Solution:

$225

If you're paying extra-super close attention, this problem is already done for you! Note that the amount of money that Gina spent on charity is equal to the amount of money that she had left, because the money that remains after her Caribbean vacation is split in half: one part to charity and the other part she hasn't spent. Since Gina had $225 left, she spent $225 on her charity.

Let's say you missed that, or you want to practice working the problem out anyway. Think abut how the remaining $225 relates to the fractional part of money spent. Gina spent 1/5th of her paycheck on her vacation, which left her with 4/5 of her paycheck remaining. She then spent half of the remaining 4/5 (which is 1/2 • 4/5), or 2/5 of her paycheck. Therefore, what remains is another 2/5 of her paycheck.

$\dfrac{2}{5} \bullet x = 225$, where x stands for her paycheck

$\dfrac{5}{2}(\dfrac{2}{5} \bullet x = 225)$ Multiply both sides of the equation by $\dfrac{5}{2}$ to solve for x

$x = 562.50$

So, she donated $\dfrac{1}{2}$ of $\dfrac{4}{5}$ of 562.50 $= \dfrac{1}{2} \bullet \dfrac{4}{5} \bullet 562.50 = 225$.

Tool #2: Familiarize yourself with common types of word problems.

A. Distance Word Problems

For distance problems, use the formula:

$$\text{Distance} = \text{Rate} \bullet \text{Time}$$

Example 7.3

Dara drove 500 miles over 12 hours. For the first leg of her trip, Dara drove 40 miles an hour for 240 miles. What was her average rate of travel for the remainder of her trip?

Solution:

43⅓

Fill in the given information:

	Distance	Rate	Time
First leg	240	40	?
Second Leg	?	?	?

Then, use the given information to fill in the remainder of the chart:

1) The distance of the first leg is 240 miles at a rate of 40 miles per hour. Using Distance = Rate • Time, you can find that the time is 6 hours. That leaves 6 remaining hours for the second leg.

2) The total distance traveled is 500 miles. Since 240 were driven in the first leg, then the remaining 260 miles were driven in the second leg.

3) Since the distance of the second leg is 260 miles driven over the remaining 6 hours, the average speed for the second leg was 43⅓ miles per hour (found by 260/6= 43⅓) .

	Distance	Rate	Time
First leg	240	40	6
Second Leg	260	**43⅓**	6

When introducing variables for multiple unknowns, choose a variable for one of the unknowns, and then base the other unknowns off of that one variable. For example, if the total trip took 12 hours, and the first leg took x hours, the rest of the trip took 12-x hours. (Use 12-x instead of introducing a new variable y.)

Example 7.4

Shannon commuted one hour total to and from work yesterday. She rode her bike to work in the morning at 10 miles per hour but got a flat tire so she walked home at 4 miles per hour that evening. How far is her house from her job?

Solution:

$\dfrac{20}{7}$ miles

Let x represent the time it takes to get to work. The time it takes to get home is equal to the total time (1 hour) less the time it takes to get to work (x parts of an hour). Thus the return trip is represented by (1-x).

	Distance	Rate	Time
To Work	?	10	x
To Home	?	4	1-x

Since d=r•t, multiply the rate and time columns to get the values in the distance column.

	Distance	Rate	Time
To Work	10x	10	x
To Home	4(1-x)	4	1-x

Given the context of the problem, set the distances equal to each other: the distance to work equals the distance to home.

$10x = 4(1-x)$

$10x = 4 - 4x$

$\underline{+4x \qquad +4x}$

$14x = 4$

$$\frac{14x}{14} = \frac{4}{14}$$

$x = \dfrac{2}{7}$ of an hour to get to work

To find the distance, plug the time and rate of either leg of the trip into the distance formula:

$$d = r \bullet t$$

$$d = 10 \bullet \frac{2}{7} = \frac{20}{7}$$

B. Work Word Problems

If multiple people (or machines) are completing a job together (say, building houses or binding books), the formula to determine how fast each is working or how long the job will take to complete is determined by the **work formula**, where the sum of the product of each entity's rate of work and the duration of that work is equal to the completion of the job.

Work Formula:

Rate$_1$ • Time$_1$ + Rate$_2$ • Time$_2$ = 1,

where 1 stands for one complete job

For example, if a person can complete a job in 12 hours, his rate is $\frac{1}{12}$ of the job per hour. That is, he can complete $\frac{1}{12}$ of the job in an hour. If he works for 5 hours, he can complete $\frac{1}{12} \bullet 5$ or $\frac{5}{12}$ of the job. If he works for x hours, he can complete $\frac{1}{12} \bullet x$ or $\frac{x}{12}$ of the job. And finally, if a person can complete a job in x hours, his rate is $\frac{1}{x}$ of the job per hour. If he works for 2 hours, he can complete $\frac{1}{x} \bullet 2$ or $\frac{2}{x}$ of the job.

Example 7.5

Irene can shovel a driveway in 5 hours. Demetrius can shovel a driveway in 4 hours. Working together at a constant pace, how long would it take the two of them to shovel half of the driveway? (At which point, they go in for a hot chocolate break?)

Solution:

$\dfrac{10}{9}$ **hours**

Irene's rate is $\dfrac{1}{5}$ of the work per hour. Demetrius' rate is

$\dfrac{1}{4}$ of the work per hour. Let's say that they work for x hours:

$\dfrac{1}{5} \bullet x + \dfrac{1}{4} \bullet x = \dfrac{1}{2}$ (where $\dfrac{1}{2}$ stands for half of the job)

$\dfrac{4}{20}x + \dfrac{5}{20}x = \dfrac{1}{2}$ Get a common denominator on the left side of the equation.

$\dfrac{9}{20}x = \dfrac{1}{2}$

$\dfrac{20}{9}\left(\dfrac{9}{20}x = \dfrac{1}{2}\right)$ Solve for x by multiplying by the reciprocal of $\dfrac{9}{20}$

$x = \dfrac{10}{9}$

It will take $\dfrac{10}{9}$ of an hour for Irene and Demetrius to shovel half the driveway.

Example 7.6

Ken can clean the house in 4 hours. If he and his wife Mary Ann take 1.5 hours to complete the job together, how long would it take Mary Ann to clean the house by herself?

Solution:

$2\dfrac{2}{5}$

Ken's rate of work is $\dfrac{1}{4}$ of the work per hour. His wife's rate of work is $\dfrac{1}{x}$ of the work per hour.

$$\dfrac{1}{4} \bullet 1.5 + \dfrac{1}{x} \bullet 1.5 = 1$$

$$\dfrac{1.5}{4} + \dfrac{1.5}{x} = 1$$

$$\dfrac{1.5x}{4x} + \dfrac{6}{4x} = 1 \quad \text{Get a common denominator.}$$

$$\dfrac{1.5x + 6}{4x} = 1 \quad \text{Add fractions.}$$

$1.5x + 6 = 4x \quad$ Multiply both sides of the equation by 4x.

$6 = 2.5x \quad$ Subtract 1.5x from both sides.

$$\dfrac{6}{2.5} = \dfrac{2.5x}{2.5} \quad \text{Isolate x by dividing both sides by 2.5.}$$

$$2\dfrac{2}{5} = x$$

160

It will take Mary Ann $2\frac{2}{5}$ hours to clean the house by herself.

C. Age Word Problems

For age problems, set up a chart that relates the age of one person at a particular time to that of others. Only use one variable and base everyone else's age off of that variable. And remember, "x" years ago means that the person is x years younger, and "y" years from now means that the person is y years older.

For example, if Norma is 56 years old, 8 years ago she was 48 years old, x years ago she was (56-x) years old, and in m years she will be (56+m) years old.

Example 7.7

Six years ago, Carolyn was five more than three times Rosalind's age. Three years from now, Carolyn will be two more than twice Rosalind's age. How old is Carolyn now?

Solution:

15 years old

Let x represent Rosalind's age 6 years ago. It is easier to base the variable off of Rosalind's age, since Carolyn's age is based on Rosalind's age.

Ages	Six Years Ago	Now	Three Years From Now
Carolyn	$3x + 5$	$(3x+5) + 6$	$[(3x+5) + 6] + 3$
Rosalind	x	$x + 6$	$x + 9$

Note that the problem mentions the past (six years ago) and the future (in three years) but if you also include their ages in the present, it helps you keep track of their ages in the future.

Now, set up an equation to solve for x, given that in three years Carolyn will be 2 more than twice Rosalind's age:

$[(3x + 5) + 6] + 3 = 2(x + 9) + 2$ In three years, Carolyn's age will be two more than twice Rosalind's age

$[(3x + 5) + 6] + 3 = 2x + 18 + 2$ Distribute the 2 on the right side of the equation.

$$3x + 14 = 2x + 20$$ Simplify.

$$\underline{-3x \qquad -3x}$$ Subtract 3x from both sides.

$$14 = -1x + 20$$

$$14 = -1x + 20$$

$$\underline{-20 \qquad -20}$$ Subtract 20 from both sides.

$$-6 = -1x$$

$$\frac{-6}{-1} = \frac{-1x}{-1}$$ Divide both sides by negative 1.

$$6 = x$$

Since Carolyn is now $(3x + 5) + 6$, she is $3 \cdot 6 + 5 + 6 = 29$.

D. Mixture Word Problems:

Mixture problems come in different forms. You might be asked how to mix investments, solutions, or ingredients in order to get the balance desired—or what portion of each ingredient went into a mixture to achieve a certain balance. Even though they come in different forms, the principle underlying mixture problems is the same, and can often be solved with a version of the following formula (note that this formula only includes two inputs but can be extended to include more):

$$\text{Quantity Input}_1 \cdot \% \text{ Concentration}_1 + \text{Quantity Input}_2 \cdot \% \text{ Concentration}_2 =$$
$$\text{Sum of Quantities of Inputs} \cdot (\text{Overall \%Concentration})$$

The formula above might sound like gibberish, so let's do a few examples.

Example 7.8

Michelle is making a snack mix for her party. She feels guilty that she is attending a potluck and not actually cooking a dish, so instead of simply buying a snack mix, she is mixing her own from two existing mixes. She desires a mix that is half pretzels. The first mix has 40% pretzels. The second mix has 70% pretzels. What is the ratio of Mix 1 to Mix 2 needed in order to create a 40-ounce mix of 50% pretzels?

Solution:

2

Let's say that Michelle uses x ounces of Mix 1. The rest of the 40 ounces, which is 40 minus how many ounces of Mix 1 she used (or, 40-x) must be of Mix 2.

	Quantity	Pretzel Concentration	Ounces of Pretzels
Mix 1	x ounces	40%	40% • x
Mix 2	(40-x) ounces	70%	70% • (40-x)
Total	40 ounces	50%	50% • 40

The sum of the ounces of the pretzels in Mix 1 and in Mix 2 is equal to the total number of ounces of pretzels: 40%x + 70%(40-x) = 50%(40).

$.4x + 28 - .7x = 20$

$$-.3x + 28 = 20$$
$$\underline{-28 \quad -28}$$
$$-.3x \quad = -8$$

$$\frac{-.3x}{-.3} = \frac{-8}{-.3}$$

$$\frac{-.3x}{-.3} = \frac{-8}{-.3}$$

$$x = 26\frac{2}{3} \text{ ounces}$$

Thus, Michelle needs $26\frac{2}{3}$ ounces of Mix 1 and $40 - 26\frac{2}{3}$ ($13\frac{1}{3}$) ounces of Mix 2.

The ratio is $26\frac{2}{3} : 13\frac{1}{3} = 2 : 1 = 2$.

Example 7.9

Matt is investing $12,000 in two bonds, one with a 5% yield and the other with an 8% yield, each compounded annually. If Matt earns $720 in interest, how much did he invest in the bond with the higher yield?

Solution:

$4,000

164

	Amount invested	% Yield	Interest
Bond 1	x	5%	5% • x
Bond 2	12,000-x	8%	8% • (12,000-x)
Total	12,000	--	720

$$5\%x + 8\%(12,000 - x) = 720$$

$$.05x + 960 - .08x = 720$$

$$-.03x + 960 = 720$$
$$ - 960 \qquad -960$$
$$\frac{-.03x}{-.03} = \frac{-240}{-.03}$$

$$x = 8,000$$

Since $8000 was invested at 5%, the remaining $4000 was invested at 8%, the higher yielding bond.

CHAPTER 7 PRACTICE SET:

1) Sean ran at a steady pace for 26.2 miles in four hours and six minutes. What was his approximate pace per mile?

a) 9 minutes and 23 seconds

b) 9 minutes and 38 seconds

c) 9 minutes and 39 seconds

d) 10 minutes and 6 seconds

e) 10 minutes and 45 seconds

2) Keith takes 3 hours to rake the leaves and Kevin takes 2 hours to do the same job. Working together, how many hours will it take them to rake the leaves?

a) 1.2

b) 2.4

c) 2.5

d) 3.0

e) 5.0

3) Two trains, both traveling southbound, are running on parallel tracks. Train A runs at 100 miles per hour and Train B runs at 120 miles per hour. If Train A leaves the station at 9 a.m., and Train B leaves the station at 11 a.m., at what time does Train B catch up to Train A?

a) 6 p.m.

b) 7 p.m.

c) 8 p.m.

d) 9 p.m.

e) 10 p.m.

4) Carlos had 3 times as much money as John until he gave John half of his money. After the exchange, what was the ratio to Carlos' money stash to John's?

a) 1:3

b) 2:3

c) 3:5

d) 5:3

e) 3:1

5) Tonya set aside 5% of her income to invest. Of this 5%, she invested 80% in a bond with a 4% return and 20% in a bond with a 6% return. What was Tonya's average return on her investment?

a) 4.0%

b) 4.4%

c) 5.0%

d) 5.2%

e) 6.0%

6) Five years ago, Kelsey was half of her brother's age. Her brother is now five years less than twice her age. How old could her brother be?

Indicate **all** ages that apply.

a) 18

b) 25

c) 32

d) 33

e) 34

7) James needs a solution that is 10% sodium. However, the only two mixtures available are 5% and 12% sodium. What is the ratio of 5% solution to 12% solution needed to reach the 10% balance?

a) 1:2

b) 2:5

c) 3:5

d) 5:7

e) 5:12

8) Due to its growing employment sector, New City experienced a population surge of 5% last year to 112,000 residents. Approximately how many residents did New City have before the surge?

SOLUTIONS: Chapter 7 Practice Set

1) a
2) a
3) d
4) c
5) b
6) a, b, c, d, and e
7) b

8) 106, 667

EXPLANATIONS: Chapter 7 Practice Set

1) **a**

This is a rate question in which we need to find minutes/mile.

First, convert the total time to 246 minutes. (To convert hours into minutes, multiply the number of hours by 60).

Then, divide the time (in minutes) by the distance (in miles) to get the minutes/mile: 246 minutes/26.2 miles = roughly 9.389 minutes.

Finally, convert .389 minutes into seconds: .389 • 60 = 23 seconds.

Sean's approximate pace per mile is 9 minutes and 23 seconds.

2) **a**

In one hour, Keith can do $\frac{1}{3}$ of the job and Kevin can do $\frac{1}{2}$ of the job.

In x hours, Keith and do $x \cdot \frac{1}{3}$ of the job and Kevin can do $x \cdot \frac{1}{2}$ of the job:

$$x \cdot \frac{1}{3} + x \cdot \frac{1}{2} = 1,\text{ where 1 stands for one complete job.}$$

$$\frac{1}{3}x + \frac{1}{2}x = 1$$

$$\frac{2}{6}x + \frac{3}{6}x = 1$$

$$\frac{5}{6}x = 1$$

$$\frac{6}{5}(\frac{5}{6}x)=\frac{6}{5}\bullet 1$$

$$x=\frac{6}{5}=1.2$$

Also note that none of the other answers make sense. If it takes Kevin 2 hours to do the job working alone, once he gets help, the job will take fewer than 2 hours.

3) **d**

	Distance	Rate	Time
Train A	100x	100	x
Train B	120(x-2)	120	x-2

When Train B catches up to Train A, the two trains will have traveled the same distance. Therefore, their distances can be set equal to each other:

$100x = 120(x-2)$

$100x = 120x - 240$

$$\begin{array}{rl} 100x &= 120x - 240 \\ -120x & -120x \\ \hline -20x &= -240 \end{array}$$

$$\frac{-20x}{-20} = \frac{-240}{-20}$$

$x = 12$

Thus, Train B caught up to Train A at 9 p.m., 12 hours after Train A left.

4) **c**

Let Carlos have $300 to John's $100. Carlos gave John half of his money ($150), which left Carlos with $150 and John with $250. The ratio, then, is 150: 250, which reduces to 3:5.

Alternatively, let Carlos' stash be $3x to John's $x. Carlos gives John $1.5x, leaving Carlos with $1.5x and John with $2.5 x.

The ratio, then, is 1.5x: 2.5x, which simplifies to 3:5:

1.5x: 2.5x

3x : 5x   Multiply both sides of the ratio by 2

3 : 5   Divide both sides of the ratio by x

5) **b**

Note that the fact that Tonya set aside 5% of her income is irrelevant in this problem, as the question asks about the average return on the money she invests—not on her total income. Thus, we needn't be concerned with the total money she invests.

Let x stand for the total amount of money that Tonya invests.

	Amount invested	% Yield	Interest
Bond 1	80%x	4%	3.2% • x
Bond 2	20%x	6%	1.2% • x
Total invested	x	--	4.4% • x

The return, as indicated in the final box, is 4.4%—the sum of the individual returns.

Alternatively, assume Tonya set aside a particular dollar amount, like $100. She would have invested $80 at 4% for a return of $3.20 and $20 at 6% for a return of $1.20. Her total return on investment, then, is $4.40, or 4.4% of the $100 she invested.

6) **a, b, c, d, e**

Let x represent Kelsey's brother's age five years ago. He is now (x+5) years old. Kelsey's age five years ago is then (1/2)x and is currently (1/2)x+5.

	Five years ago	**Now**
Kelsey	1/2 • x	1/2 • x + 5
Brother	x	x+ 5

Kelsey's brother is now five years less than twice her age:

$$2(\frac{1}{2} \cdot x + 5) - 5 = x + 5$$

$$x + 10 - 5 = x + 5$$

$$x + 5 = x + 5$$

$$x = x$$

This identity indicates that this relationship holds no matter what Kelsey's brother's age is. Thus, her brother could be any age.

7) **b**

Percent sodium	Number of ounces	Amount of sodium
5% solution	x	.05x
12% solution	y	.12y

In this problem we could not avoid introducing a second variable because we were not given a total number of ounces. However, in this problem we are asked for the relative amount of each solution needed as opposed to the actual amount.

Since the amount of sodium at 5% solution is .05 x and the amount of solution at 12% solution is .12y, and the total amount of sodium at 10% is .10(x+y), our initial equation can be written as follows:

$.05x + .12y = .10(x + y)$

$.05x + .12y = .10x + .10y$

$.02y = .05x$ Subtract both sides by .10y and .05x to get terms on separate sides.

$\dfrac{.02y}{.05} = \dfrac{.05x}{.05}$ Solve for x by dividing both sides by .05.

$.4y = x$ Divide both sides by y to get in ratio form of x / y.

$\dfrac{x}{y} = .4 = \dfrac{4}{10} = \dfrac{2}{5}$

8) **106,667**

$112,000 = 105\%$ of pre-surge population

Let x = pre-surge population

$112,000 = 105\%x$

$112,000 = 1.05x$

$$\frac{112,000}{1.05} = \frac{1.05x}{1.05}$$

$x = 106,667$ (rounded)

Chapter 8: Let Me Get This Straight

(Lines and Angles)

A line has 180 degrees. If you split a line into multiple angles, the sum of those angles adds to 180 degrees. Below, the sum of Angle 1 and Angle 2 is 180 degrees (m<1 + m<2 = 180), because their non-shared sides form a straight line.

(Note: m<1 stands for "the measure of angle 1".)

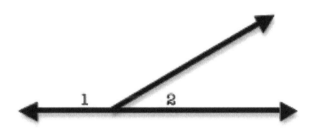

An **acute** angle measures less than 90 degrees (like <2 above).

An **obtuse** angle measures more than 90 degrees (like <1 above).

A **right angle** measures exactly 90 degrees.

Example 8.1

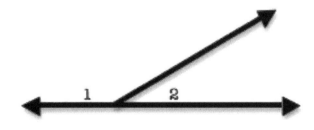

a) If m<1 is 3.5 times the m<2, what is the m<1?

b)If m<1 is 30 degrees more than the m<2, what is m<2?

c) If m<1= 3x+40 and the m<2= x^2 + 100, what is/are the value(s) of x?

Solution:

a) **140 degrees**

Since m<1 is 3.5 times the m<2, if m<2 is x then m<1 is 3.5x.

Thus, x + 3.5x= 180.

$$x + 3.5x = 180$$
$$\frac{4.5x}{4.5} = \frac{180}{4.5}$$

$$x = 40$$

So the measure of <2 is 40 degrees and the measure of <1 is 180-40 = 140 degrees.

b) **m<2= 75 degrees**

Let m<2= x. Then m<1=x+30, and x+x+30=180. Thus 2x+30=180, and x=75. The m<2= 75 degrees.

c) **x= 5 or -8**

$$3x + 40 + x^2 + 100 = 180$$

$$\begin{array}{r} x^2 + 3x + 140 = 180 \\ -180 \quad -180 \\ \hline x^2 + 3x - 40 \;=\; 0 \end{array}$$

$$(x + 8)(x - 5) = 0$$

By the Zero Product Property :

$$x + 8 = 0 \qquad \text{or} \qquad x - 5 = 0$$
$$\underline{-8 \quad -8} \qquad\qquad \underline{+5 \ +5}$$
$$x = -8 \qquad\qquad x = 5$$

Two intersecting lines form 4 angles. The angles opposite each other are **congruent**, meaning they have equal measures. The angles **adjacent** (or next to) each other, add to 180 degrees. (You can see that any two adjacent angles formed by intersecting lines fall along a straight line.)

In the diagram below, m< 1 = m< 3 and m< 2 = m< 4. Each set of adjacent angles adds to 180 degrees. For example, m <1 + m <2= 180 degrees.

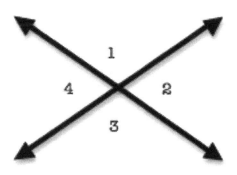

Example 8.2

a) Based on the intersecting lines above, if m<1 = 2x and m<2 = 3y, what is the m<3 in terms of y?

b) If m<2= 5x, what is the average of measures of <1, <2, <3, and <4?

Solution:

a) **m<3= 180-3y**

177

Since m<1 + m<2= 180, 2x + 3y = 180. Since m<3 is also 2x, solve the equation for 2x, which results in 2x=180-3y.

b) **90 degrees**

Note that it is not necessary to have any information about the individual angles, because you are being asked to find the average. The sum of the angles is 360 degrees, and there are 4 angles: average= sum/# = 360/4 = 90.

Parallel Lines:

Note: The following properties apply ONLY to parallel lines.

Two parallel lines cut by a third line (a **transversal**) form eight angles.

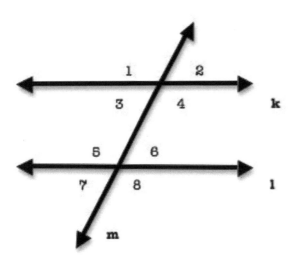

If one of the angles is 90 degrees, all of the angles are 90 degrees.

If there are no 90 degree angles, then four of the angles are acute and the other four angles are obtuse.

All of the acute angles are equal and all of the obtuse angles are equal. The sum of any acute angle and any obtuse angle is 180 degrees.

Given that lines k and l above are parallel (which either has to be stated explicitly or indicated by the parallel symbols: >) and cut by a third line m, angles 2, 3, 6, and 7 are congruent and angles 1, 4, 5, and 8 are congruent.

Example 8.3

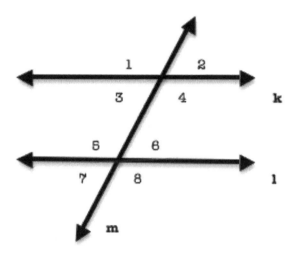

Given parallel lines k and l above,

a) If m<1= 2x+ 15 and m<5= 125, what is x?

b) If m<1= 7x+ 15 and m<7= 25, what is x?

Solution:

a) **55**

First note that the set of lines are parallel. Since both angles are obtuse, they are congruent:

$$2x + 15 = 125$$
$$\underline{\quad -15 \quad -15 \quad}$$
$$2x \quad = 110$$

$$\frac{2x}{2} = \frac{110}{2}$$

$$x \quad = 55$$

b) **20**

First note that the set of lines are parallel. Since <1 is obtuse and <7 is acute, the angles sum to 180 degrees: 7x+ 15 + 25 = 180.

$$7x + 15 + 25 = 180$$
$$7x + 15 + 25 = 180$$
$$7x + 40 \quad = 180$$
$$\underline{\quad -40 \quad \quad -40 \quad}$$
$$7x \quad = 140$$

$$\frac{7x}{7} = \frac{140}{7}$$

$$x = \quad 20$$

CHAPTER 8 PRACTICE SET:

1)

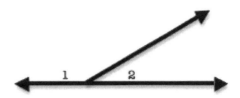

The m<2 above is 40 degrees less than m<1. What is the m<1?

2)

Given two parallel lines k and l cut by a transversal, if m<1= u and the m<6= 2p+7, what is the the value of p in terms of u?

a) 7-2u

b) (173-u)÷2

c) (u+ 7)÷2

d) (u-7)÷2

e) 2u+7

3)

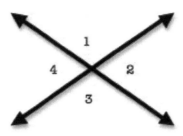

If m<4 is 82 degrees, what is the positive difference, in degrees, between m<1 and m<2?

4)

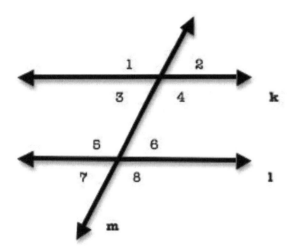

If m<3 = x + 12, and m<7= 2x-9, what is the value of x?

a) 7

b) 21

c) 59

d) 83

e) Cannot be determined

5)

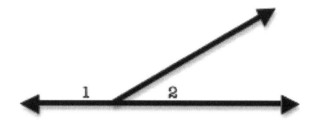

The m<2 above is 80 degrees less than 3 times the m<1. If the m<1 is x, which of the following represents the difference of the angles in terms of x?

a) -2x-80

b) -2x+80

c) -80-4x

d) 4x - 80

e) 2x+ 80

SOLUTIONS: Chapter 8 Practice Set

1) 110
2) b
3) 16
4) e
5) b

EXPLANATIONS: Chapter 8

1) **110 degrees**

Let m<2= x. Then m<1= 40 + x.

m<1 + m<2 = 180

$$40 + x + x = 180$$

$$40 + 2x = 180$$

$$-40$$

$$\overline{\qquad\qquad 2x = 140}$$

$$\frac{2x}{2} = \frac{140}{2}$$

$$x = 70$$

m<1 = 70 + 40 = 110 degrees

2) **b**

The m<1 + m<6=180 (since lines l and k are parallel, and <1 is acute and <6 is obtuse): u+2p+7= 180.

$$u + 2p + 7 = 180$$
$$\underline{\qquad -7 \quad -7}$$
$$u + 2p = 173$$

Work to isolate the variable p by subtracting 7 and then variable u from both sides of the equation.

$$u + 2p = 173$$
$$\underline{-u \qquad\qquad -u}$$
$$2p = 173 - u$$

Divide both sides of the equation by 2.

$$\frac{2p}{2} = \frac{173 - u}{2}$$

$$p = \frac{173 - u}{2}$$

3) **16**

Since <1 and <2 are adjacent, their measures sum to 180 degrees. And since m<2 = m<4 (because they are vertical angles), m<2= 82 degrees. 180-82= 98=m<1. The difference, then, is 98-82=16.

4) **e**

The value of x cannot be determined because, although the lines appear to be parallel, we are not told that they are.

5) **b**

If m<1 is x, then m<2 is 3x-80. The difference, then, is:

x - (3x-80)

x-3x-(-80)

-2x+80

Chapter 9: Shape Up!

(Triangles and Other Polygons)

Triangle Facts:

The **perimeter** of a triangle is the sum of the lengths of its sides.

The **area** of a triangle is 1/2•base•height.

The shortest side of a triangle is across from the smallest angle; the longest side is across from the largest angle.

The sum of the interior angles of a triangle is 180 degrees.

The length of a side of a triangle must be greater than the difference of the other two sides and less than the sum of the other two sides.

For example, if the lengths of the sides of a triangle are 8, 12, and x, then x must be greater than the difference and less than the sum of the other two sides: 12-8<x<12+8, or 4<x<20.

Example 9.1: If two sides of a triangle are 12 and 13, what is the sum of the smallest and greatest possible integer lengths of the third side?

a) 1
b) 2
c) 25
d) 26
e) 27

Solution: d

The third side must be between the difference and sum of the two known sides: 13-12< x < 12 + 13.

Thus, 1<x<25. Since x is an integer, the shortest the length can be is 2 and the longest the length can be is 24. The sum, then, is 26.

Special Triangles:

An **isosceles triangle** has two sides of equal length and the two angles opposite those sides are **congruent** (meaning, have the same measure).

An **equilateral triangle** has all equal angles and all equal side lengths.

The formula for the area of an equilateral triangle is:

$$\frac{s^2 \sqrt{3}}{4}$$

, where s is the length of the side of the triangle.

Example 9.2

If the perimeter of an isosceles triangle is 48 cm, what could be the lengths of two of the sides of the triangle?

Indicate <u>all</u> that apply.

a) 6 and 36
b) 8 and 20
c) 10 and 28
d) 14 and 17
e) 14 and 20
f) 15 and 18
g) 16 and 20

Solution: b, d, e, and f

The perimeter must sum to 48, and the missing side must be the same length as one of the known sides (since the triangle is isosceles).

In addition, the lengths of the sides must preserve the relationship that the sum of 2 sides is greater than the third, and the difference of two sides is less than the third.

In answer choice b, the missing side could be 20. In answer choice d, the missing side could be 17. In answer choice e, the missing side could be 14. In answer choice f, the missing side could be 15.

In answer choice a, the missing side length could be 6, but the sum of side lengths 6 and 6 is not greater than the third side length of 36. In answer choice c, to get a perimeter of 48, the missing side length would have to be

10. However, the two short sides of 10 and 10 do not have a sum greater than the third side of 28. In answer choice g, there is no length that we can add that will make the triangle isosceles with perimeter of 48.

A **right triangle** has exactly one right angle (90 degrees) and two acute angles. The triangle below has right angle C.

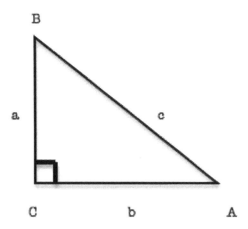

If you know the lengths of two sides of a right triangle, you can find the length of the third side by using the following theorem:

> **Pythagorean Theorem**: $a^2 + b^2 = c^2$, where a and b are the lengths of two sides and c is the length of the **hypotenuse**, the side opposite the right angle.

Special Right Triangles:

45-45-90 Triangles (or **isosceles right triangle**)

Right triangles that have two congruent angles are 45-45-90 triangles. The ratios of the measures of their sides are $x:x:x\sqrt{2}$.

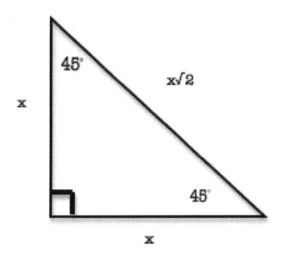

Check-ins:

1) In a 45, 45, 90 degree triangle, if one of the legs is 8, what is the length of the hypotenuse?

2) In an isosceles right triangle, if the hypotenuse is 8, what is the length of each leg?

Solutions:

1) hypotenuse: 8√2

The length of the legs are 8 in this isosceles right triangle. Since the ratio in a 45-45-90 is x:x:x√2, x=8 and the hypotenuse of x√2 is 8√2.

2) leg: $4\sqrt{2}$

In an isosceles right triangle, the ratio again is $x:x:x\sqrt{2}$. Since the hypotenuse of $x\sqrt{2}$ is 8, divide 8 by $\sqrt{2}$ to get x:

$$x\sqrt{2} = 8$$

$$\frac{x\sqrt{2}}{\sqrt{2}} = \frac{8}{\sqrt{2}}$$

$$x = \frac{8}{\sqrt{2}}$$

$$x = \frac{8 \cdot \sqrt{2}}{\sqrt{2} \cdot \sqrt{2}} = \frac{8\sqrt{2}}{2} = 4\sqrt{2} \quad \text{Rationalize the denominator.}$$

Example 9.3

If the shorter sides of an isosceles right triangle is $5\sqrt{2}$, what is its perimeter?

Solution:

$10 + 10\sqrt{2}$

An isosceles right triangle has lengths in the ratio of $x:x:x\sqrt{2}$. The short sides are represented by length x which, in this case, is $5\sqrt{2}$. Therefore, the sides of this triangle are $5\sqrt{2}$, $5\sqrt{2}$, and $5\sqrt{2} \cdot \sqrt{2}$.

The perimeter is $5\sqrt{2} + 5\sqrt{2} + 5\sqrt{2} \cdot \sqrt{2}$, which simplifies to $10\sqrt{2} + 10$.

30-60-90 Triangles

For right triangles that have angle measurements of 30, 60, and 90 degrees, the ratio of the measures of their sides is x: x√3:2x.

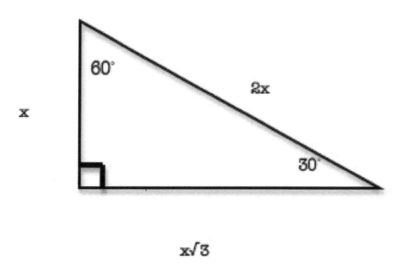

Check-in:

In a 30, 60, 90 degree triangle, if the hypotenuse is 10, what are the lengths of the other sides?

Solution:

shorter side: 5, longer side: 5√3

The hypotenuse is 10. Since the ratio in a 30-60-90 is 1x:√3x:2x, 2x=10. Therefore, x=5, and √3x= 5√3.

Example 9.4

Given that two triangles have the same hypotenuse, which has the greater area: a 30-60-90 or a 45-45-90?

Solution:

The 45-45-90 triangle has the greater area.

Choose a length for the hypotenuse, say 8, and find the area of each triangle using the formula: A= 1/2 • b • h.

Find the side lengths of the 30:60:90, given the ratio of x: x√3: 2x. 2x= 8, so x=4 and x√3= 4√3. The area, then, is: (1/2)• 4 • 4√3=8√3.

Find the side lengths of the 45:45:90, given the ratio of x: x: x√2. x√2 = 8, so x=8/√2 or 4 √2. The area, then, is: (1/2)• 4√2 • 4√2=16. Since 16> 8√3, the area of the 45-45-90 triangle is greater.

Polygons

A **polygon** is a closed, flat figure with at least three straight lines.

Examples of polygons are triangles, rectangles, pentagons, and octagons. Note that the **perimeter** of any polygon is the sum of the lengths of its sides.

Area of Polygons:

Rectangle: base • height

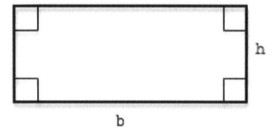

b

Square: s^2

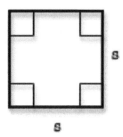

Parallelogram: base • height

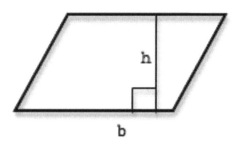

Trapezoid: $(1/2)(b_1+b_2)$ • h

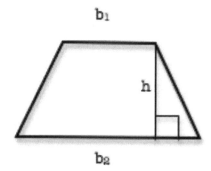

Note that a trapezoid has two bases, denoted b_1 and b_2.

The **sum of the measures of the interior angles** of a polygon is equal to: $(n-2)$ • 180 degrees, where n represents the number of sides of the polygon.

The **exterior angles** of a polygon always sum to 360 degrees, irrespective of the number of sides of the polygon.

A **regular** polygon has all equal sides AND all equal angle measures.

Example 9.5

How many sides does a figure have if the sum of the measure of its interior angles is 900 degrees?

a) 5

b) 6

c) 7

d) 8

e) 9

Solution: c

Set 900 equal to the formula for the sum of the measures of the interior angles of a polygon formula and solve for n:

$(n-2) \bullet 180 = 900$

$180n-360 = 900$

$\underline{ +360 +360}$

$180n = 1260$

$n = 7$

CHAPTER 9 PRACTICE SET:

Use the following figure to answer 1-3:

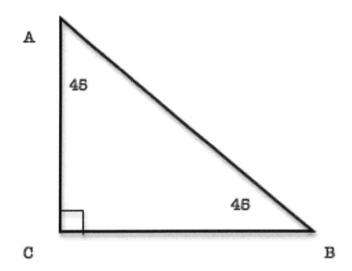

1) If AB is $3\sqrt{2}$, what is the area of the right triangle above?

a) 4.5

b) 9.0

c) 13.5

d) 18.0

e) 18.5

2) If AB is 3, what is the perimeter of the right triangle above?

a) $3\sqrt{2}$

b) $3\sqrt{2} + 3$

c) $3\sqrt{2} + 6$

d) $9\sqrt{2}$

e) $9\sqrt{2} + 6$

3) If the perimeter of triangle ABC above is 8 + 4√2, what is the length of AC?

Use the following figure to answer 4-6:

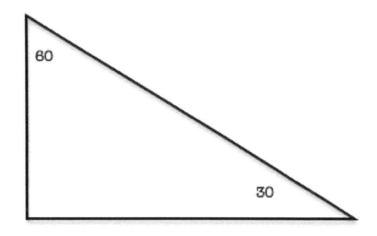

4) If the shortest side is 8, what is the area of the triangle?

a) 32

b) 64

c) 32√2

d) 32√3

e) 64√3

5) If the longer leg is 3mn, what is the ratio of the length of the shorter side to the hypotenuse?

Write answer as a fraction.

6) What is the perimeter of the figure if the hypotenuse has a measurement of length z?

a) $(\frac{1}{2} + \sqrt{3})z$

b) $(\frac{3}{2} + \sqrt{3})z$

c) $(\frac{1}{2} + \frac{\sqrt{2}}{2})z$

d) $(\frac{3}{2} + \frac{\sqrt{3}}{2})z$

e) $(3 + \sqrt{3})z$

7) If two sides of a triangle are 8 and 10, what is the greatest possible integer length of its perimeter?

a) 18

b) 27

c) 28

d) 35

e) 36

Use the following figure to answer 8 and 9:

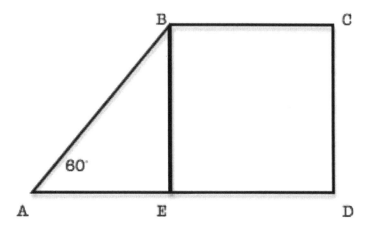

8) Given that BCDE is a square, and the length of AE is 8, what is the perimeter of figure ABCDE?

a) $8 + 24\sqrt{3}$

b) $32 + 8\sqrt{3}$

c) 40

d) $24 + 24\sqrt{3}$

e) $48 + 16\sqrt{3}$

9) Given that BCDE is a square, and the length of AE is 8, what is the area of figure ABCDE?

a) $32 + 32\sqrt{3}$

b) $32 + 8\sqrt{3}$

c) 64

d) $64 + 32\sqrt{3}$

e) $192 + 32\sqrt{3}$

10)

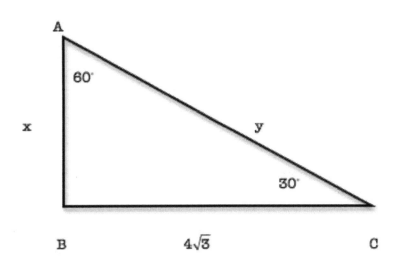

A
60°

x

y

30°

B   4√3   C

Quantity A   Quantity B

The ratio of y to x   2

11)

Quantity A   Quantity B

Probability that a right   Probability that a right triangle
triangle has at least one   has at least one acute angle
obtuse angle

12) A figure has 1,620 interior degrees. If the average of 6 of the angles is 125, what is the average of the remaining angles?

a) 147
b) 154
c) 162
d) 169
e) 174

SOLUTIONS: Chapter 9 Practice Set

1) a
2) b
3) 4
4) d
5) 1/2
6) d

7) d

8) d

9) e

10) c

11) b

12) e

EXPLANATIONS: Chapter 9

1) **a**

Area is 1/2•b•h. Note that the hypotenuse is $3\sqrt{2}$, so each leg is 3.
Substituting 3 in for the base and height, then, gives us: 1/2•3•3= 4.5.

2) **b**

If AB is 3, then the legs are $3/\sqrt{2}$. The perimeter, then, is:

$$\frac{3}{\sqrt{2}}+\frac{3}{\sqrt{2}}+3$$

$$\frac{6}{\sqrt{2}}+3 \qquad\qquad\qquad \text{Rationalize the denominator.}$$

$$\frac{6}{\sqrt{2}}\bullet\frac{\sqrt{2}}{\sqrt{2}}+3 \;=\frac{6\sqrt{2}}{2}+3= 3\sqrt{2}+3$$

3) **4**

The perimeter of an isosceles triangle is: $x + x + x\sqrt{2}$.

$$x + x + x\sqrt{2} = 8 + 4\sqrt{2}$$
$$= 4 + 4 + 4\sqrt{2}$$

Thus, x=4. AC=4.

4) **d**

The ratio of the lengths of the sides are x, $x\sqrt{3}$, and 2x.

The shorter leg is the shortest side, which is x=8.

The longer leg is the second shortest side, which is $x\sqrt{3} = 8\sqrt{3}$.

The area, then, is: $8 \bullet 8\sqrt{3} \bullet 1/2 = 32\sqrt{3}$.

5) **1/2**

The ratio of the shortest side to the hypotenuse in a 30-60-90 triangle is always 1 to 2, irrespective of the length of any of the sides, because the ratio of the sides is x:2x. Alternatively, calculate the length of the shorter side and the length of the hypotenuse and find the ratio.

6) **d**

The ratio of the sides of a 30-60-90 triangle are $1:\sqrt{3}:2$. If the longest side (the hypotenuse) is z, then the shortest side is (1/2)z and the middle length side is $(1/2)z\sqrt{3}$. The sum is:

$$\frac{1}{2}z + \frac{1}{2}z\sqrt{3} + 1z = \frac{3}{2}z + \frac{1}{2}z\sqrt{3} = (\frac{3}{2} + \frac{\sqrt{3}}{2})z$$

7) **d**

The length of a side of a triangle must be between the sum and difference of the lengths of the other two sides of the triangle:

$10-8 < x < 10 + 8$

$2\ < x <\ \ 18$

Therefore, the greatest integer length of the third side is 17, making the greatest perimeter integer length: 8 + 10 + 17 = 35.

8) **d**

The length of BE is $8\sqrt{3}$ because it is the side opposite the 60 degree angle (and the side opposite the 30 degree angle is 8). Therefore, the sides of the square are $8\sqrt{3}$.

In addition, the length of the hypotenuse is 16 (again, because the side opposite the 30 degree angle is 8). Thus, the perimeter is: $8\sqrt{3} \cdot 3 + 8 + 16 = 24 + 24\sqrt{3}$.

9) **e**

As explained in problem 8, the length of BE is $8\sqrt{3}$. The area of the square, then, is $b \cdot h = 8\sqrt{3} \cdot 8\sqrt{3}$. The area of the triangle is $1/2 \cdot 8 \cdot 8\sqrt{3}$.

The area of the figure, then, is: $8\sqrt{3} \cdot 8\sqrt{3} + 1/2 \cdot 8 \cdot 8\sqrt{3} = 192 + 32\sqrt{3}$

10) **c**

Since this is a 30-60-90 triangle, the ratio of y to x is 2 to 1, regardless of the lengths of the sides. Alternatively, find the value of y (which is 8) and the value of x (which is 4). The ratio of y:x is 8:4, which reduces to 2:1.

11) **b**

Since the angle measures of triangles add up to 180 degrees, if one of the angles of a triangle is a right angle (90 degrees), the sum of the measures of the other two angles must add up to the remaining 90 degrees. Thus, both of the non-right angles must be acute.

Therefore, the probability in Quantity A is 0 and the probability in Quantity B is 1.

12) **e**

To find the average of the remaining angles, you must know both the sum of the remaining angles and the number of the remaining angles:

$$\text{Average} = \frac{\text{Sum}}{\text{\# of Numbers}}$$

To find the sum, subtract the sum of the first six angles from the total of 1,620. The sum of the first six angles is $125 \bullet 6 = 750$ (found by multiplying the given average by the number of angles).

This difference is $1,620 - 750 = 870$.

To find the total number of angles, set the formula for the total number of interior degrees of a polygon equal to the total of 1,620 degrees.

$$(n-2)180 = 1,620$$

$$\frac{(n-2)180}{180} = \frac{1,620}{180}$$

$$n-2 \quad = 9$$
$$n \quad\quad = 11$$

Since there are 11 total angles, there are 5 remaining angles (after subtracting 6 angles from the total).

Finally, to find the average of the remaining angles, divide the remaining degrees by the remaining angles:

$$\text{Average} = \frac{870}{5} = 174$$

(Circles)

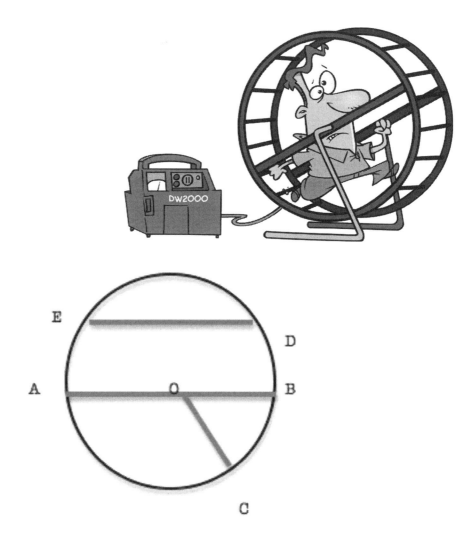

Circles are 360 degrees around. The **radius** of a circle is any line segment from the center (denoted above by O) to a point on the circle. OB, OC, and OA are radii. All radii are equal in length. The **diameter** touches two points on the circle, passing through the center. AB is a diameter.

Because it goes through the center, the diameter is the longest **chord**, which is a line segment whose endpoints lie on the circle. DE and AB are examples of chords.

The **circumference** of a circle is $2\pi r$. The circumference is its perimeter.

The **area** of a circle is πr^2.

Arc length is part of the circumference of a circle and the **area of the sector** is part of the area of the circle.

Below are the formulas to find arc length and the area of a sector.

arc length : $\dfrac{x}{360} \bullet 2\pi r$

area of sector : $\dfrac{x}{360} \bullet \pi r^2$

where x is the measure of the central angle of the circle.

Example 10.1

If the area of a circle is 24π, what is its circumference?

Solution:

$4\sqrt{6}\pi$

Use the area formula to find the radius and then plug the value of the radius into the circumference formula.

$24\pi = \pi r^2$ 　　　　Set 24π equal to the area and then solve for r.

$\dfrac{24\pi}{\pi} = \dfrac{\pi r^2}{\pi}$ 　　　　Divide both sides by π.

$24 = r^2$ 　　　　Take the square root of both sides to isolate r.

$$\sqrt{24} = \sqrt{4} \cdot \sqrt{6} = 2\sqrt{6} = r$$

To find the circumference, plug the value of r into the circumference formula.

$$2\pi r = 2 \cdot \pi \cdot 2\sqrt{6} = 4\sqrt{6}\pi$$

Example 10.2

The ratio of the radii of two circles is 5 to 9. What is the ratio of the area of the large circle to the area of the small circle?

a) 5:9
b) 5:14
c) 25:81
d) 9:5
e) 81:25

Solution:

e

The area of the larger circle is 81π and the area of the smaller circle is 25π, so the ratio is 81:25.

Also note that, even without calculating the areas, the answer could only be d or e because the question asks for the ratio of the area of the larger circle to that of the smaller circle, so the first number in the ratio must be greater than the second.

Equation of a Circle

The following is the equation of the graph of a circle:

$$(x - h)^2 + (y - k)^2 = r^2$$

where (h, k) is the center of the circle and r is the radius.

Therefore, based on the following equation of a circle:

$$(x - 8)^2 + (y + 7)^2 = 9$$

the center is (8, -7) and the radius is 3.

Example 10.3

Given the following equation : $(x-2)^2 + (y+5)^2 = 7$, what is the circumference of the circle?

Solution:

$$2\sqrt{7}\pi$$

Since $r^2 = 7$, then $r = \sqrt{7}$. Substitute $\sqrt{7}$ in to the circumference formula $(2\pi r)$ to get $2\sqrt{7}\pi$.

If a line is **tangent** to a circle, it intersects the circle at exactly one point. If a radius is drawn from the center of the circle to this point of tangency, that radius is perpendicular to the tangent line.

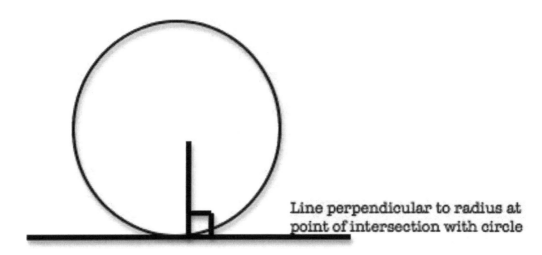

Line perpendicular to radius at
point of intersection with circle

CHAPTER 10 PRACTICE SET:

1) If the circumference of a circle is 2π, what is its area?

a) $\dfrac{1}{4}\pi$

b) $\dfrac{1}{2}\pi$

c) π

d) 2π

e) $\dfrac{5}{2}\pi$

2) If the area of a circle is 2π, what is its circumference?

a) $\sqrt{2}\pi$

b) π

c) 2π

d) $2\sqrt{2}\pi$

e) 4π

3) The radius of circle A is x and the radius of circle B is 2x, what is the ratio of the area of circle B to the area of circle A?

a) 1:2

b) 1:4

c) 2:1

d) 4:1

e) Cannot be determined

Use the following information and figure below to answer #4-6: Radius OE is 5, the m< O is 45 degrees.

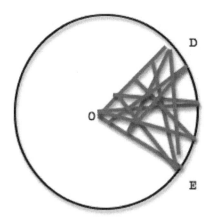

4) What is the length of arc ED in Circle O above?

a) $\dfrac{1}{4}\pi$

b) $\dfrac{1}{2}\pi$

c) $\dfrac{3}{4}\pi$

d) $\dfrac{5}{4}\pi$

e) $\dfrac{5}{2}\pi$

5) What is the area of shaded sector DOE above?

a) $\dfrac{1}{8}\pi$

b) $\dfrac{3}{8}\pi$

c) $\dfrac{9}{8}\pi$

d) $\dfrac{16}{8}\pi$

e) $\dfrac{25}{8}\pi$

212

6) If the area of the unshaded sector above is pπ, what is p? Give your answer to the nearest 0.1

7) For what length radius is the area of a circle equal to twice its circumference?

a) 1

b) √2

c) 2

d) 2√2

e) 4

8) Two concentric circles A (larger) and B (smaller) have radii of 12 and 8 respectively. What is the positive difference of their areas?

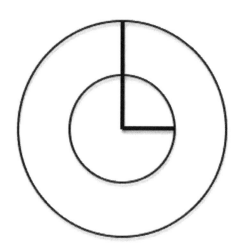

a) 4π

b) 16π

c) 64π

d) 80π

e) 144π

9) In the figure below, <B is tangent to the circle with center C. The area of Circle C is how many times π?

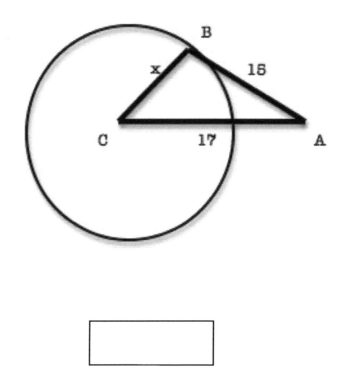

SOLUTIONS: Chapter 10 Practice Set

1) c
2) d
3) d
4) d
5) e
6) 21.9
7) e
8) d
9) 64

EXPLANATIONS: Chapter 10 Practice Set

1) **c**

Use the circumference formula to find the radius, then plug the value of the radius into the area formula.

$2\pi r = 2\pi$ Set circumference formula equal to 2π.

$\dfrac{2\pi r}{2\pi} = \dfrac{2\pi}{2\pi}$ Solve for r (by dividing both sides by 2π).

$r = 1$ Simplify.

$\pi r^2 = \pi(1)^2 = \pi$ Input the value of r into the area formula.

2) **d**

Use the area formula to find the radius, then plug the value of the radius into the circumference formula.

$\pi r^2 = 2\pi$

$\dfrac{\pi r^2}{\pi} = \dfrac{2\pi}{\pi}$

$r^2 = 2$

$\sqrt{r^2} = \sqrt{2}$

$r = \sqrt{2}$

$2\pi r = 2\pi\sqrt{2}$

3) **d**

The area of circle A is: πr^2 $= \pi x^2$

The area of circle B is: πr^2 $= \pi(2x)^2 = \pi 4x^2$

The ratio of the areas of circle B to circle A, then, is:

$4\pi x^2 : \pi x^2$

4   :   1

4) **d**

$$\frac{x}{360} \cdot 2\pi r = \frac{45}{360} \cdot 2\pi(5)$$

$$= \frac{1}{8} \cdot 10\pi$$

$$= \frac{10}{8} \cdot \pi$$

$$= \frac{5}{4} \cdot \pi$$

5) **e**

$$\frac{x}{360} \cdot \pi r^2 = \frac{45}{360} \cdot \pi(5)^2$$

$$= \frac{1}{8} \cdot 25\pi$$

$$= \frac{25}{8}\pi$$

6) **21.9**

Total area - shaded sector area = unshaded sector area

$$25\pi - \frac{25}{8}\pi = \frac{200}{8}\pi - \frac{25}{8}\pi = \frac{175}{8}\pi$$

So, p is $\frac{175}{8}$, or roughly 21.9.

7) **e**

$\pi r^2 = 2(2\pi r)$ Translate the sentence.

$\pi r^2 = 4\pi r$ Simplify.

$r^2 = 4r$ Divide both sides by π.

$r = 4$ Divide both sides by r.

8) **d**

Area of big circle : $\pi r^2 = \pi(12)^2 = 144\pi$

Area of small circle $\pi r^2 = \pi(8)^2 = 64\pi$

Difference : $144\pi - 64\pi = 80\pi$

9) **64**

Since AB is tangent to Circle C, the triangle is a right triangle. The unknown length of the right triangle is the radius of the circle. In order to find the unknown length of the side (and therefore the radius of the circle), use the Pythagorean Theorem:

$$x^2 + 225 = 289$$
$$\underline{ - 225 \quad -225}$$
$$x^2 \qquad = \quad 64$$

$$x \qquad = \quad 8$$

Since the length of x is also the length of the radius, use the formula for the area of a circle ($A=\pi r^2$) to find that the area of the circle is 64π. Thus, the area is 64 times π.

Chapter 11: 3-D

(Solid Figures)

The keys to solving solid geometry figure problems on the GRE are:

1) knowing the formulas, and

2) figuring out how what you are being asked relates to one (or more) of the formulas.

Commonly Tested 3D Shapes:

Remember that **volume** is the measure of the capacity of a three-dimensional object, and **surface area** is the sum of the areas of each face of a three-dimensional object.

Rectangular Prism :

l stands for length, w stands for width, and h stands for height

Volume : $l \bullet w \bullet h$ **Surface area :** $2(l \bullet h + w \bullet h + w \bullet l)$

Length of the longest diagonal : $\sqrt{l^2 \bullet w^2 \bullet h^2}$

Cube :

e stands for the length of an edge

Volume : e^3 **Surface area :** $6e^2$

Cylinder :

Volume : $\pi r^2 h$

Lateral Surface Area : $2\pi rh$
(does not include top or bottom faces)

Surface Area : $2\pi rh + 2\pi r^2$
(includes top and bottom faces)

Example 11.1

Shana is filling a cubic bathtub that is 2 feet long. After one cubic foot flows into the tub:

a) What percent of the tub is filled?
b) How high does the water reach?

Solution:

a) **12.5 percent**

Since it is a cubic bath tub, the dimensions are 2x2x2. The tub therefore has a capacity of 8 cubic feet. Since 1 cubic foot has flowed into the tub, 1/8 or 12.5% of the tub is filled.

b) $\dfrac{1}{4} \text{ft}$

This is a question about dimensions based on volume. Note that 1 cubic foot has flowed into the tub, so the volume is 1 cubic foot. Using the formula for volume (l•w•h), we can determine the height:

$$l•w•h = 2•2•h = 1$$
$$4h = 1$$
$$h = \frac{1}{4}$$

Example 11.2

Quantity A	Quantity B
Surface area of rectangular prism with dimensions 12•2•2	Surface area of rectangular prism with dimensions 6•4•4

Solution:

b

Calculate the surface area of each.

Quantity A: 2[(12•2 + 2•2 + 12•2)]= 104
Quantity B: 2[(6•4 + 4•4 + 6•4)]= 128

Note that you can also compare the two without working out a full calculation. 12•2 = 24, as does 6•4. The only difference, then, is the 2•2 in Quantity A versus the 4•4 in Quantity B.

Example 11.3

If the dimensions of a box are 8 by 12 by 4, what is the length of the longest item, with negligible width and height, that could fit in the box? Answer to the nearest 0.1 of an inch.

Solution:

Imagine that the item lies along the longest diagonal of the box, then use the formula for the length of the longest diagonal of a rectangular prism:

$$\sqrt{l^2 + w^2 + h^2} = \sqrt{8^2 + 12^2 + 4^2} = \sqrt{224},\text{ which is approximately } 15.0.$$

CHAPTER 11 PRACTICE SET:

Refer to the figure below for #1-4:

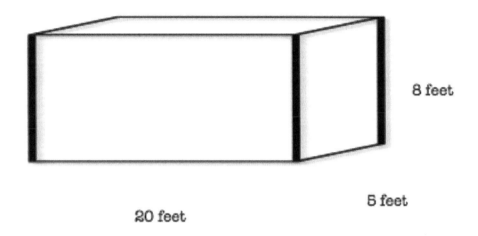

8 feet

5 feet

20 feet

1) What is the volume of the figure in cubic inches?

2) How many buckets of paint are needed to paint the rectangular prism
above, given that one bucket of paint covers 75 square feet?

3) What is the total surface area, in square units, of the two figures that
result if the figure above is cut in half along its depth (so that there are two
rectangular prisms of depth 2.5 feet each instead of one of depth 5 units)?

4) What is the length of the longest diagonal of the figure to the nearest foot?

5) The cylinder below has a diameter of d units and a height of h units, where h= 4d. What is the volume of the cylinder in terms of d?

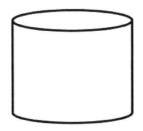

a) $\frac{1}{4}d^2\pi$

b) $\frac{1}{4}d^3\pi$

c) $d^3\pi$

d) $4d^2\pi$

e) $4d^3\pi$

6) Cylinder A, which has a radius of 5 mm and a height of 8 mm, is filled with water. Cylinder B, which has a radius of 12 mm and a height of 9 mm, is empty. If half of the water from Cylinder A is poured into Cylinder B, what fractional part of Cylinder B is full?

a) $\dfrac{25}{324}$

b) $\dfrac{50}{324}$

c) $\dfrac{75}{324}$

d) $\dfrac{100}{324}$

e) $\dfrac{150}{324}$

SOLUTIONS: Chapter 11 Practice Set

1) 1,382,400
2) 8
3) 920
4) 22
5) c
6) a

EXPLANATIONS: Chapter 11 Practice Set

1) **1,382,400**

First convert each dimension into inches by multiplying by 12, because the dimensions are given in feet, but the question asks for inches:

l: $20 \bullet 12 = 240$ inches

w: $5 \bullet 12 = 60$ inches

h: $8 \bullet 12 = 96$ inches

Then plug the values into the volume formula:

$V = l \cdot w \cdot h = 240 \cdot 60 \cdot 96 = 1,382,400$ in^3.

2) **8**

This question requires you to find the surface area of the rectangular prism:

$2(l \cdot w + l \cdot h + h \cdot w)$

$2(20 \cdot 5 + 20 \cdot 8 + 8 \cdot 5) = 600$ ft^2.

Since one bucket covers 75 ft^2, we would need 8 buckets: $600 \div 75$.

3) **920**

By cutting the figure in half along its depth, you create two $20 \cdot 2.5 \cdot 5$ rectangular prisms. Since the resulting prisms have the same dimensions, find the surface area of one, and then double it to get the total surface area of both prisms:

Surface area of a single prism:
$2(l \cdot h + h \cdot d + d \cdot l) = 2(20 \cdot 8 + 8 \cdot 2.5 + 2.5 \cdot 20) = 460$.

So, the total surface area of both figures is $2 \cdot 460$, or 920 feet^2.

4) **22**

$\sqrt{(20^2+5^2+8^2)} = \sqrt{489} = 22.11$.

To the nearest whole number, the longest diagonal is 22 ft long.

5) **c**

Volume of a cylinder: $\pi r^2 h$.

Since, $r = (1/2) \cdot d$ and $h = 4d$:

$\pi r^2 h = \pi(\frac{1}{2}d)^2(4d)$

$\qquad = \frac{1}{4}d^2(4d)\pi$

$= d^3 \pi$

6) **a**

Volume of Cylinder A: $\pi r^2 h = 200\pi$ mm^3

Volume of Cylinder B: $\pi r^2 h = 1296\pi$ mm^3

Half of the water from Cylinder A is poured into Cylinder B, making Cylinder B $100\pi/1296\pi$ full, which reduces to $25/324$.

Chapter 12: Gettin' Down to the Nitty Grid-dy

(Coordinate Geometry)

A coordinate plane, as shown below, is made of two perpendicular number lines whose intersection, **the origin**, falls at zero on each line.

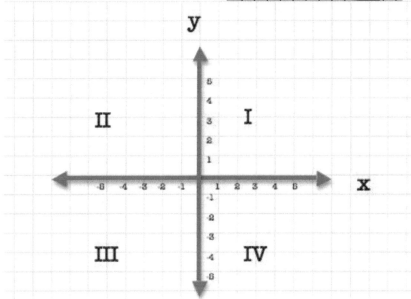

Each point on a coordinate plane corresponds to an ordered pair (x, y), where the x coordinate determines horizontal movement (left for negative values and right for positive values) from the origin and the y coordinate determines vertical movement (down for negative values and up for positive values) from the origin.

The quadrants (numbered I through IV) are marked above.

Any two points on a coordinate grid determine a line.

Example 12.1

A point is located in the second quadrant. Which of the following could be true about the product of the coordinates of the ordered pair associated with the point?

Select **all** answer choices that apply.

a) product > 0
b) product < 0
c) product = 0

Solution:

b

If a point is located in the second quadrant, the x coordinate is negative and the y coordinate is positive. Therefore, the product of its coordinates is negative.

Slope:

The **slope** of a line is the measure of its vertical change relative to its horizontal change. If a line is graphed, you can calculate the slope by identifying two points on the line and counting the "rise" (the vertical change from point one to point two) over the "run" (the horizontal change from point one to point two).

The formula for **slope (m)**, given points (x_1, y_1) and (x_2, y_2) is :

$$\frac{y_2 - y_1}{x_2 - x_1}$$

Check-in:

Find the slope of the lines that go through the following points:

a) $(2,3)$ and $(5,8)$ b) $(-2,7)$ and $(8,-9)$

c) $(3,5)$ and $(8,5)$ d) $(8,9)$ and $(8,3)$

Solution:

a) $\dfrac{5}{3}$ b) $\dfrac{-8}{5}$

$\dfrac{8-3}{5-2} = \dfrac{5}{3}$ $\dfrac{-9-7}{8-(-2)} = \dfrac{-16}{10} = \dfrac{-8}{5}$

c) **0**   d) **undefined**

$\dfrac{5-5}{8-3} = \dfrac{0}{5} = 0$ $\dfrac{3-9}{8-8} = \dfrac{-6}{0} \rightarrow$ undefined slope

The slope is:

positive- if the line is increasing from left to right

negative- if the line is decreasing from left to right

zero- if the line is horizontal

undefined- if the line is vertical

Two lines are parallel if they do not intersect. Parallel lines have the same slope, but different y-intercepts (the point where the line crosses the y axis).

Two lines are **perpendicular** if their slopes are the negative reciprocals of each other. For example, 2/3 and -3/2 are slopes of perpendicular lines. The product of perpendicular lines is -1. For example: 2/3 • -3/2= -1.

Distance Formula:

The distance between two points can be found using the Pythagorean Theorem. Consider the two points (x_1, y_1) and (x_2, y_2). The distance between the two points is d. Find the length of the horizontal leg, which is the change in the x coordinates (x_2-x_1) and the length of the vertical leg, which is the change in the y coordinates (y_2-y_1). Then, plug this into the Pythagorean Theorem formula and you have the **Distance Formula:**

$$d = \sqrt{(x_2 - x_1)^2 + (y_2 - y_1)^2}$$

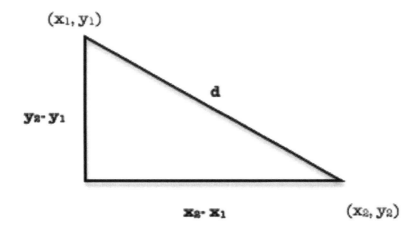

Check-in:

Find the distance between the following sets of points:

a) $(2,3)$ and $(5,8)$ b) $(8,9)$ and $(8,3)$

Solution:

a) $\mathbf{3\sqrt{5}}$

$$\sqrt{(5-2)^2 + (8-3)^2} = \sqrt{(3)^2 + (5)^2} = \sqrt{34} = \sqrt{34}$$

b) $\mathbf{6}$

$$\sqrt{(8-8)^2 + (3-9)^2} = \sqrt{(0)^2 + (-6)^2} = \sqrt{36} = 6$$

Example 12.2

Chandra left her home to head for the grocery store. She walked .8 miles east and .4 miles north. She then realized that she forgot to drop off her library books, so she went 1.0 mile south. At this point, how many miles was Chandra from home?

a) 0.8
b) 1.0
c) 1.2
d) 1.4
e) 2.2

Solution:
b

Chandra is .8 miles east and .6 miles south of her home. (She initially went .4 miles north, but after going south for one mile from that point, she was ultimately .6 miles south). Using the Pythagorean Theorem (or distance formula), we find that Chandra is one mile from home:

$.8^2 + .6^2 = \text{distance}^2$

$.64 + .36 = 1$

Take the square root of 1, which is 1, to find Chandra's distance from home.

Midpoint Formula:

The **midpoint** of a line segment is the ordered pair that corresponds to the middle of the line segment. The x coordinate of the midpoint is found by taking the average of the x coordinates of the endpoints and the y coordinate of the midpoint is found by taking the average of the y coordinates of the endpoints:

$$\left(\frac{x_1 + x_2}{2} , \frac{y_1 + y_2}{2} \right)$$

Check-in:

Find the midpoint of the line segment with endpoints (2, 5) and (8, -7).

Solution:

(5,-1)

233

Graphing Lines in Two Variables:

An equation in the form y= mx + b is said to be in **slope intercept form**, where m is the slope and b is the y-intercept.

To graph a line in slope intercept form, first graph the **y-intercept** (the point where the line crosses the y axis, at which point x= 0). From the y-intercept, count the rise over the run as indicated by the slope to get a second point on the line.

For example, the graph of y= 1x-3 (see graph below) has a y-intercept of -3 and a slope of 1 (that is, for every point you "rise," you must "run" one to the right).

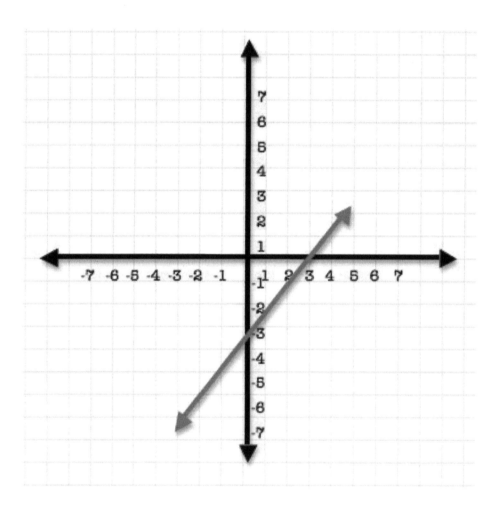

Alternatively, when given the graph of a line, you can work backwards to determine the equation of that line by 1) identifying the y-intercept (b) and 2) identifying the slope (m).

Then, plug those values for m and b into the equation y=mx+b.

Example 12.3

Find the equation of the line graphed below.

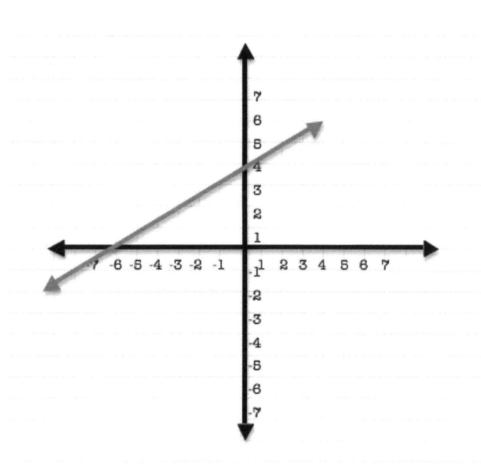

Solution:

$$y = \frac{2}{3}x + 4$$

Step 1: Note that the graph crosses the y axis at y = 4. This is the y-intercept, or the b.

Step 2: Identify two of the points on the line. For example, (-6, 0) and (0,4).

Step 3: Find the slope based on the two points found in Step 2, either by using the slope formula or counting the rise and the run from one point to the next.

Step 4: Since y = mx+ b, plug in the found values for m and b:

$$y = \frac{2}{3}x + 4$$

Graphing Inequalities in Two Variables:

You graph inequalities similarly to the way you graph equations, with two differences:

1) If the inequality has a < or >, the line graphed is a dashed line. (If the inequality has a ≤ or ≥, the graphed line is still solid.)

2) For an inequality, the solution set includes both the line (≤ or ≥) and shading above or below the line. For example, in the inequality y ≥ 2x + 3, both the line and all points above the line (since y is "GREATER THAN or equal to") make the statement true.

To confirm where the shaded area should be, find a "test" point, which is any point not on the graphed line. Input the values of the test point into the inequality. If the resulting inequality is true, shade to include the test point. If the resulting inequality is false, shade AWAY from the point on the other side of the line.

See Example 12.4 for clarity.

Example 12.4

What is the graph of the inequality below?

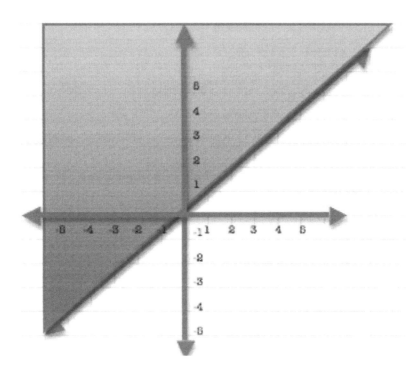

Solution:

y ≥ x

The y-intercept of the graph below is y=0, because the graph crosses the y axis at (0,0). The slope is 1/1 (found by counting up 1 unit for every 1 unit moved to the right). And, since y is greater than or equal to x, the shading must go above the line.

Alternatively, to determine the shading, take a test point, say (-1, 2). Substitute this test point into the inequality y ≥ x: 2 ≥ -1. Since this is a true statement, shade above the line to include the point (-1, 2).

If you had tested a point below the line, like (2,0), you would have gotten the statement: 0 ≥ 2, which is not true. Since this is not true, you must shade on the other side of the line, away from the test point.

Functions:

Coordinate planes are also used to graph **functions** [often denoted by f(x)], which show relationships between an input (x) and its unique output (y).

Functions can be defined as rules, such as: f(x) = 2x + 3, where the inputs, (x) and the outputs (f(x)) can be plotted as ordered pairs (x,f(x)) on a coordinate plane.

.

To find a given value of f(x) based on a specific value of x, substitute the value of x into the function and simplify.

Example 12.5

a) If $f(x) = 3x + 6$, what is f(x) when $x = \dfrac{2}{3}$?

b) If $f(x) = x - 9$ and $g(x) = \dfrac{x}{3}$, what is f(g(x))?

Solution:

a) **8**

Simply substitute $\dfrac{2}{3}$ in for x :

$$f(\tfrac{2}{3}) = 3(\tfrac{2}{3}) + 6 = 2 + 6 = 8$$

b) $\dfrac{\textbf{x-27}}{\textbf{3}}$

G(x) is the input to function f(x). Therefore, substitute $\dfrac{x}{3}$ (which is g(x)) in for x in the function f(x) :

$$g(x) = (\tfrac{x}{3}) \text{ so } f(g(x)) = f(\tfrac{x}{3}) = \tfrac{x}{3} - 9 = \tfrac{x}{3} - \tfrac{27}{3} = \tfrac{x-27}{3}$$

Functions in the form of :

$f(x) = ax + b$ are lines

$f(x) = ax^2 + bx + c$ are parabolas

Shifting Functions

If a function $f(x)$ is graphed, it can be shifted as follows:

$f(x) + c$ means shift up c units

$f(x) - c$ means shift down c units

$f(x+c)$ means shift left c units

$f(x-c)$ means shift right c units

Example 12.6

Given function $f(x) = (x+3)^2$, which of the following functions represents $f(x)$ being shifted 5 units down and 6 units to the left?

a) $f(x) = (x-5)^2 + 6$
b) $f(x) = (x+5)^2 - 6$
c) $f(x) = (x-6)^2 - 5$
d) $f(x) = (x+6)^2 + 5$
e) $f(x) = (x+9)^2 - 5$

Solution:

e

A shift of 5 units down and 6 units to the left means:

$f(x+6) - 5 = ((x+6)+3)^2 - 5 = (x+9)^2 - 5$

CHAPTER 12 PRACTICE SET:

1) For what value of k would the following two lines be perpendicular?

$3x + 2y = 12$ and $4x - ky = 4$

a) $-\dfrac{8}{3}$

b) $-\dfrac{3}{8}$

c) $\dfrac{2}{3}$

d) $\dfrac{3}{2}$

e) $\dfrac{6}{1}$

2) Which of the following ordered pairs is a solution to: $2x - 8y = 16$ and

$\dfrac{1}{4}x - y = 2$?

Select **all** that apply:

a) (0, -2)

b) (4, -1)

c) (6, -1/2)

d) (14, 3/2)

Use the figure below to answer questions #3-6.

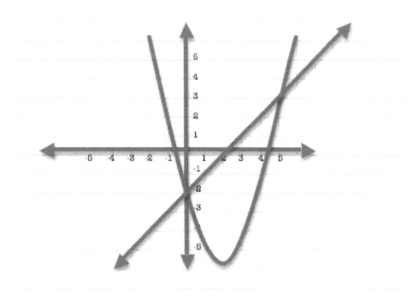

3) What is the midpoint of the line segment whose endpoints lie on the parabola?

a) (-2.0, -0.5)

b) (-1.5, 0.5)

c) (1.5, -0.5)

d) (2.5, 0.5)

e) (5.0, 1.0)

4) What is the closest approximation of the length of the line segment whose endpoints lie on the parabola?

a) 7.0

b) 7.5

c) 8.0

d) 8.5

e) 9.0

5) What is the slope of a line that is perpendicular to the line shown?

a) -1.0

b) -0.5

c) 0.0

d) 0.5

e) 1.5

6) If the original parabola $f(x)$ had its vertex at the origin, which of the following represents its current position?:

a) $f(x+2)-6$

b) $f(x-2)-6$

c) $f(x-2)+6$

d) $f(x-6)+2$

e) $f(x+6)-2$

7) $f(x) = x^3$, $g(x) = \sqrt{f(x)}$, what is the value of $g(x)$ when $x = \dfrac{1}{4}$?

SOLUTIONS: Chapter 12 Practice Set

1) e
2) a, b, c, d
3) d
4) a
5) a

6) b

7) $\dfrac{1}{8}$

EXPLANATIONS: Chapter 12 Practice Set

1) **e**

If two lines are perpendicular, their slopes are the negative reciprocals of each other. Write each equation in slope intercept form:

Equation 1 :

$$3x + 2y = 12$$

$$\underline{-3x \qquad\qquad -3x}$$

$$2y = 12 - 3x$$

$$\frac{2y}{2} = \frac{12 - 3x}{2}$$

$$y = 6 - \frac{3}{2}x$$

$$y = -\frac{3}{2}x + 6$$

Equation 2 :

$$4x - ky = 4$$

$$\underline{-4x \qquad\qquad -4x}$$

$$-ky = -4x + 4$$

$$\frac{-ky}{-k} = \frac{-4x + 4}{-k}$$

$$y = \frac{4}{k}x + \frac{4}{-k}$$

The slopes of the two lines, then are $\frac{-3}{2}$ and $\frac{4}{k}$. The slope of $\frac{4}{k}$, then, must be the negative reciprocal of $\frac{-3}{2}$, which is $\frac{2}{3}$:

$$\frac{4}{k} = \frac{2}{3}$$

$$12 = 2k$$

$$k = 6$$

2) **a, b, c, d**

243

If you write both equations in slope-intercept form, you will find that they both simplify to the same equation, y= (1/4)x-2. Therefore, any solution to this equation is a solution to both original equations.

3) **d**

The line segment whose endpoints lie on the parabola are: (0, -2) and (5, 3).

$$\frac{x_1 + x_2}{2} = \frac{0+5}{2} = 2.5$$

$$\frac{y_1 + y_2}{2} = \frac{-2+3}{2} = .5$$

$$(2.5, .5)$$

4) **a**

The line segment whose endpoints lie on the parabola are: (0, -2) and (5, 3).

To find the length of a line segment, use the distance formula:

$$\sqrt{(x_2 - x_1)^2 + (y_2 - y_1)^2} = \sqrt{(0-5)^2 + (-2-3)^2} = \sqrt{25+25} = \sqrt{50} \approx 7.0.$$

5) **a**

The slope of the line shown can be found by using the slope formula, calculating the change in y values over the respective change in x values.

Using the points (0, -2) and (5, 3):

$$\frac{3-(-2)}{5-0} = 1$$

The slope of a line perpendicular to the one shown, then, is -1 (which is the negative reciprocal of 1).

Note that a line perpendicular to the line shown must have a negative slope. So, even without calculating the slope, the only reasonable answer choices would be a) and b).

6) **b**

The graph above is shifted two units to the right and six units down.

7) $\dfrac{1}{8}$

Since $f(x) = x^3$, when $x = \dfrac{1}{4}$: $f(\dfrac{1}{4}) = (\dfrac{1}{4})^3 = \dfrac{1}{64}$.

Therefore, $g(\dfrac{1}{4}) = \sqrt{f(\dfrac{1}{4})} = \sqrt{\dfrac{1}{64}} = \dfrac{1}{8}$.

Chapter 13: What're the Odds? (Counting and Probability)

Student: "If I study for the GRE every day during commercial breaks of Law & Order re-runs, what is the probability that I will ace the test?"

The Revised GRE puts added emphasis on statistics questions, as graduate school course work often requires students to engage in statistical analysis. This chapter focuses on the main statistical concepts that appear on the GRE.

Counting:

Consider the following questions:

1) Lara sold tickets numbered 132 through 185 at the fair booth. How many tickets did she sell?

2) Sam lost weight, going from 185 to 132 pounds. How many pounds did she lose?

3) Carla is 132nd in line and her mother is 185th. How many people are between them?

These three questions each sound simple. But, when read together, you might question your answer for each.

Instead of memorizing a formula or spending a lot of time reasoning these out, plug a closer set of numbers in for the spread out ones and answer the question based on the new set of numbers. Figure out how you got the answer, and then apply this process to the original question with the original numbers.

For example, here are the questions again, but 132 has been replaced with 10 and 185 with 12. (This way you can count the answers out- even using your fingers, if you so choose).

1) Lara sold tickets numbered 10 through 12 at the fair booth. How many tickets did she sell? **Solution: 3**

2) Sam lost weight, going from 12 to 10 pounds. How many pounds did she lose? **Solution: 2**

3) Carla is 12th in line and her mother is 10th. How many people are between them? **Solution: 1**

We can quickly compute the answers above without hesitation when the numbers are close.

Next, think about what you did for each question. (Note: The initial step is always subtracting. Then consider whether you added 1, subtracted 1, or did neither). For the first question, we subtracted the numbers and then added one. For the second question, we simply subtracted the numbers. And for the third question, we subtracted the numbers and subtracted one more.

Now, return to the original questions and make sure you get the following answers: **1) 54   2) 53 3) 52**

247

Fundamental Counting Principle:

If there are 12 renditions of your favorite song "Baby, I Love You" and eight karaoke bars in the area, how many different ways do you have of embarrassing yourself?

All-important questions like these can be answered using the **Fundamental Counting Principle**, which tells us: If you have x ways of doing one thing and y ways of doing another, you have x • y different ways of doing both things. The Fundamental Counting Principle extends to any number of categories.

Example 13.1

Mia was going for lunch at The City Cheesecakery. If the Cheesecakery offers 5 different sandwiches, 3 different types of chips, 4 kinds of beverages, and 12 different cheesecake options, how many different meal combinations did Mia have to choose from if she were to have one item per category?

Solution:
720

5 choices of sandwich • 3 choices of chips • 4 choices of beverages • 12 choices of cheesecake.

Probability

Probability is defined as the number of favorable outcomes divided by the total possible outcomes:

$$\frac{\text{favorable outcomes}}{\text{all possible outcomes}}$$

Example 13.2 If there are 8 green marbles, 2 blue marbles, and 3 yellow marbles in a jar, what is the probability of randomly choosing one yellow marble?

a) $\dfrac{1}{13}$

b) $\dfrac{2}{11}$

c) $\dfrac{3}{13}$

d) $\dfrac{3}{10}$

e) $\dfrac{1}{3}$

Solution: c

There are 3 yellow marbles out of 13 total marbles. (This is an easy question but can be confusing when the word "one" is used. Students sometimes think the answer is 1/13. But there are three ways to choose that one marble of interest.)

Example 13.3 For any given right triangle, what is the probability that one of the angles will be obtuse?

a) 0

b) $\dfrac{1}{4}$

c) $\dfrac{1}{3}$

d) $\dfrac{1}{2}$

e) Cannot be determined

Solution: a

A right triangle, by definition, has one 90 degree angle. That means that the other two angles sum to 90 degrees, since there are 180 degrees in the interior of a triangle. Since 90 degrees has to be split among the remaining two angles, both angles must be acute. Thus, there is no chance that there will be an obtuse angle in a right triangle.

Simple and Compound Probability

Simple probability measures the likelihood of a single event occurring. (For example: a) Landing on green on a spinner or b) landing on green OR red on a spinner)

For simple probability, indicated by a single event occurring, sometimes with the use of the word "or," you simply ADD the individual probabilities.

Compound probability measures the likelihood of multiple events occurring. For example, a) Landing on green AND then red on a spinner or b) landing on both green and red when spinning a spinner two times.

For compound probability, indicated by multiple events occurring and often indicated by the presence of "and," you MULTIPLY the individual probabilities.

Be sure to determine whether or not the probabilities are **independent** (meaning, the probability of an event occurring is not affected by the outcome of the preceding event). For example, the probability of flipping a coin and getting heads on the last flip of 100 flips is 1/2, regardless of the results of the first 99 flips. Coin flips are independent events.

Events can also be **dependent** (meaning that the probability of an event occurring is affected by the outcome of a preceding event). For example, imagine that there are 10 students in a room (4 girls and 6 boys). There is a 4 out of 10 chance that the student who exits is a girl. Let's say that the student who exits is indeed a girl. If a second student leaves the room before the first one returns, the probability of the second student being a girl is now only 3 out of 9, because, after the first girl leaves, there are only nine students left in the room, three of whom are girls.

Remembering the difference between "or" versus "and":

Consider the following scenario. You are sitting in a coffee shop, and your buddy asks you, "What is the probability that the next person who walks in here has red hair, **OR** pink sandals, **OR** a blue watch, **OR** spiked hair **OR** a business suit on?"

And then she asks, "What is the probability that the next person who walks in here has red hair **AND** pink sandals **AND** a blue watch **AND** spiked hair **AND** a business suit on?"

You'll notice that the first scenario has a greater probability of happening, because any one of the traits will satisfy the condition. The second scenario, though, is very specific. With each "and" is an additional criterion that must be met in order to satisfy the overall condition. Remember that when we multiply fractions (which probabilities are), our number actually gets smaller. So, it makes sense that we multiply when we have multiple "must meet" conditions, as is the case with the use of the word "and."

Example 13.4a

What is the probability of getting a red or yellow on an equally spaced pie chart with colors red, yellow, green, and blue?

Example 13.4b

What is the probability of getting a red on your first spin and a yellow on your second spin?

Solution:

13.4 a. $\dfrac{1}{2}$

We have to calculate the probability of getting red OR yellow:

$$\frac{1}{4}+\frac{1}{4}$$

13.4 b. $\dfrac{1}{16}$

We have to calculate the probability of first getting red AND then getting yellow:

$$\frac{1}{4} \bullet \frac{1}{4}$$

Example 13.5

What is the probability of flipping a coin twice and getting heads the first time and tails the second time?

Solution : $\dfrac{1}{4}$

We have to calculate the probability of getting heads AND then tails:

$$\frac{1}{2} \bullet \frac{1}{2}$$

Example 13.6

What is the probability of flipping a coin three times and getting heads at least twice?

Solution:

$\dfrac{1}{2}$

Note that getting heads at least twice means that we can get heads either two or three times. So, we have to figure out: P(2H and 1T) + P(3H).

P(HHT) +P(HTH)+ P(THH) + P(HHH)=

$$\frac{1}{8} \; + \; \frac{1}{8} \; + \; \frac{1}{8} \; + \; \frac{1}{8} \; = \; \frac{4}{8} \; = \; \frac{1}{2}$$

Combinations and Permutations

Student 1: Woo hoo!!!! I am so excited!!!! We're getting close to the end of the book!!!!

Student 2: What's with all the exclamation points?????

Do you remember factorials? A factorial, represented by an exclamation point (!), is defined as follows:
n!= n • (n-1) • (n-2) • (n-3)... • 2 • 1
For example, 4!=4 • 3 • 2 • 1

Note that 0! equals 1.

Factorials are used to help us calculate **combinations** and **permutations**. That is, we can calculate the number of ways we can take n objects and arrange them in groups of size r.

Both combinations and permutations help us figure out how many ways there are of arranging a certain number of members or items in a group.

In combinations, it is said that order does not matter. In permutations, however, it does. To remember the difference, you can associate permutations with phone numbers: If you interchange the last two

254

numbers of your friend's phone number, you might end up talking to Big Brutus by mistake. That is, changing the order of the numbers produces a different result.

On the other hand, combinations allow you to rearrange members or items within a group without changing the group itself.

The following example is designed to help you see the difference.

Scenario 1: Kevin, Sam, Joe, and Dana are racing. If the top three earn bragging rights, how many possible arrangements of the group will be so privileged?

Scenario 2: Kevin, Sam, Joe, and Dana are racing. If the winner gets $50, the second place finisher gets $20, and the third place finisher gets $10, how many different outcomes are possible?

Scenario 1 is a combinations question. Once you are in the top three, there are no further distinctions— order does not matter. Scenario 2 is a permutations question. Order matters because your place within the top three determines your prize. If you rearrange the top three, you get a different outcome.

Formulas:

Combinations (nCr):

$$\frac{n!}{r!(n-r)!}$$

where n stands for the total number of objects and r stands for the number of objects chosen at a time

Permutations (nPr):

$$\frac{n!}{(n-r)!}$$

where n stands for the total number of objects and r stands for the number of objects chosen at a time

Example 13.7 a How many ways can you choose a 4-person committee from a group of 7 people?

Example 13.7 b How many ways can you choose a president, vice president, treasurer, and secretary from a group of 7 people?

Solution:

13.7 a. **35 ways**

This is a combinations problem—$_7C_4$— because the order in which you choose your 4 members does not matter.

$$\frac{7!}{4!(7-4)!}=\frac{7!}{4!(3)!}=\frac{7 \bullet 6 \bullet 5 \bullet 4 \bullet 3 \bullet 2 \bullet 1}{4 \bullet 3 \bullet 2 \bullet 1(3 \bullet 2 \bullet 1)}=\frac{7 \bullet 5}{1}=35$$

13.7 b. **840 ways**

This is a permutations problem—$_7P_4$— because choosing, say, Tom for secretary and Sue for treasurer is different than choosing Tom for treasurer and Sue for secretary.

$$\frac{7!}{(7-4)!}=\frac{7!}{3!}=\frac{7 \bullet 6 \bullet 5 \bullet 4 \bullet 3 \bullet 2 \bullet 1}{3 \bullet 2 \bullet 1}=\frac{7 \bullet 6 \bullet 5 \bullet 4}{1}=840$$

Example 13.8: Roz is redecorating her basement. She has 8 pictures to hang but only four picture hooks, one for each wall. In how many ways can she hang four pictures?

Solution:
1,680

This is a permutations question— $_8P_4$— because, even after she chooses her 4 pictures, she can change the order in which she hangs her pictures.

Example 13.9

Jackie was preparing paint supplies for her students. She had 12 different colors, and each student chose three. How many different color combinations were possible?

Solution:

220

$_{12}C_3$— This is a combinations question. Say a student chose red, persimmon, and mauve. It doesn't matter if she chose the red and then the mauve, or the mauve and then the persimmon. She still ends up with the same combination of colors.

In a permutations question, when the n=r (say, 5 people chosen for five different jobs), the denominator becomes 0! or 1. For example, if you are asked to line up 6 students in 6 different positions, both the n (the number of students) and the r (the numbers of students chosen to be lined up) equal 6. Therefore:

$$\frac{n!}{(n-r)!} = \frac{6!}{(6-6)!} = 6!$$

Therefore, when n=r, the permutation is found by simply calculating n!

In addition, in combinatorics, if an item in your arrangement is listed more than once, you have to divide by an additional factorial of the number of times an item is repeated. See example 13.10.

Example 13.10: How many different ways can you rearrange the letters in the word OHIO?

Solution:

12

Similar to the other permutation questions, this question can be answered by calculating $_4P_4$. The n and r are the same in this case because you are taking all the letters in the word in your arrangement. However, since the letter O is repeated, you have to divide by the factorial of the number of times it is listed (2!).

CHAPTER 13 PRACTICE SET:

1) Karen is trying to decide on her outfit. She has three different choices of shirts, five different pairs of pants and two different sets of jewelry. If she may or may not wear jewelry, how many choices of outfits does she have?

a) 30

b) 45

c) 60

d) 75

e) 90

2) How many ways can you rearrange the following numbers: 3, 5, 7, 6, 2, 5, 3?

3) What is the probability that you will roll a 3 and then a 6 on a fair-sided die?

a) $\dfrac{1}{36}$

b) $\dfrac{1}{8}$

c) $\dfrac{1}{6}$

d) $\dfrac{1}{3}$

e) $\dfrac{1}{2}$

4) What is the probability of rolling a 3 or a 6 on a fair-sided die?

5) Jack has 4 pairs of black socks, 5 pairs of striped socks, and 3 pairs of argyle socks, what is the minimum number of pairs he must choose in order to ensure that he gets at least two of each pair (given that each pair is pinned together)?

6) Jeter is playing darts. If he gets a dart in the figure below, in terms of s and t, what is the probability that it lands inside the equilateral triangle but outside the square?

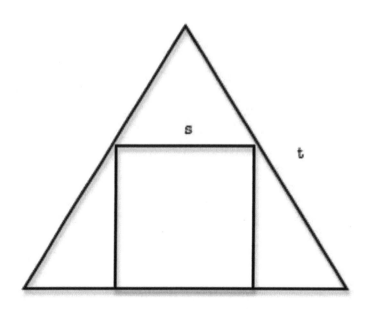

a) $\dfrac{4\sqrt{3}s^2}{3t^2\sqrt{3}}$

b) 1

c) $\dfrac{3t^2 - 4\sqrt{3}s^2}{3t^2}$

d) $\dfrac{3t^2\sqrt{3} - 4\sqrt{3}s^2}{\sqrt{3}}$

e) $\dfrac{4\sqrt{3}s^2 - 3t^2\sqrt{3}}{4\sqrt{3}s^2}$

7) At the pre-school promotion, the boys want to be next to the boys and the girls want to be next to the girls. To accommodate this request, the teachers will have the students walk in single file, with all of the girls entering the ceremony followed by each of the boys, or vice versa. If there are 4 boys and 5 girls being promoted, and either the boys or girls can go first, in how many different arrangements can the students enter the ceremony?

SOLUTIONS: Chapter 13 Practice Set

1) b
2) 1,260
3) a
4) $\dfrac{1}{3}$

5) 11
6) c
7) 5,760

EXPLANATIONS: Chapter 13 Practice Set

1) **b**

This is a Fundamental Counting Principle question with an extra step. Note that Karen may or may not wear jewelry. To take this into account, you must find out how many outfits she can make with jewelry AND how many outfits she can make without jewelry. Then add the two together.

3•5•2 (with jewelry) + 3•5 (without jewelry) = 45

2) **1,260**

There are 7 numbers, so you can arrange them 7! ways, but you have to account for the fact that two of the numbers (the 3 and the 2) are repeated: 7!/(2!•2!).

3) **a**

$P(3) \bullet P(6) = \dfrac{1}{6} \bullet \dfrac{1}{6} = \dfrac{1}{36}$ (Note that this is a compound probability question

using AND, so we must multiply.)

4) $\dfrac{1}{3}$

$\dfrac{1}{6} + \dfrac{1}{6} = \dfrac{2}{6} = \dfrac{1}{3}$ (Note that this is a simple probability question

using OR, so we must add.)

5) **11**

In order to answer this question, assume that the greatest category is exhausted first, then the next greatest category, etc, and finally, choose the minimum required (in this case, 2) from the last category.

In this case, that's 5 pairs of striped socks, 4 pairs of black socks, and 2 pairs of argyle socks.

6) **c**

First, make sure to know the definition of probability:

$$\dfrac{\text{favorable outcomes}}{\text{all possible outcomes}}$$

For geometric probability, that means:

$$\dfrac{\text{favorable area}}{\text{total area}}$$

The "favorable area" is the area we want and the "total outcome" is the total area.

The "favorable area" in this problem is found by calculating the area inside the equilateral triangle, but outside the square. And the "total area" is the area of the largest triangle:

$$\frac{\text{area of t - area of s}}{\text{area of t}}$$

To find the area of an equilateral triangle, use the formula:

$$\frac{x^2\sqrt{3}}{4}, \text{ where x is the length of the side}$$

The geometric probability, then, is:

$$\frac{\dfrac{t^2\sqrt{3}}{4} - s^2}{\dfrac{t^2\sqrt{3}}{4}}$$

Simplify the numerator by first getting a common denominator:

$$\frac{\dfrac{t^2\sqrt{3}}{4} - \dfrac{4s^2}{4}}{\dfrac{t^2\sqrt{3}}{4}}$$

Subtract the fractions in the numerator:

$$\dfrac{\dfrac{t^2\sqrt{3}-4s^2}{4}}{\dfrac{t^2\sqrt{3}}{4}}$$

Multiply by the reciprocal of the denominator (note that the "4"s cancel) and then rationalize the denominator:

$$\dfrac{t^2\sqrt{3}-4s^2}{4}\bullet\dfrac{4}{t^2\sqrt{3}}$$

$$\dfrac{t^2\sqrt{3}-4s^2}{t^2\sqrt{3}}$$

(To rationalize the denominator multiply by $\dfrac{\sqrt{3}}{\sqrt{3}}$.)

$$\dfrac{t^2\sqrt{3}-4s^2}{t^2\sqrt{3}}\bullet\dfrac{\sqrt{3}}{\sqrt{3}}=\dfrac{3t^2-4\sqrt{3}s^2}{3t^2}$$

7) **5,760**

If the boys go first, the number of permutations we can get are $4!\bullet 5!$

If the girls go first, the number of permutations are $5!\bullet 4!$.

Therefore, the total number of permutations are: $4!\bullet 5! + 5!\bullet 4! = 5{,}760$.

265

Chapter 14: Map it Out

(Data Interpretation)

For many students, graduate school is sure to include lots of graphs, charts, and data interpretation. To reflect this, the GRE now has a greater emphasis on data analysis.

The great thing about these types of questions is that many of the skills you have re-visited— like percent change and proportions— re-surface in the form of data analysis. These math skills are coupled with your reading and understanding of charts and graphs.

This chapter explores common types of data interpretation questions appearing on the GRE.

Pie Charts

Pie Charts are circle graphs that assign categories in percents relative to a whole (100%). The size of each "slice" is proportional to the whole.

Reference the pie graph below for Examples 14.1 and 14.2:

ChickKnits Yarn Sales

(Relative Profits By Quarter)

Total: $60,030

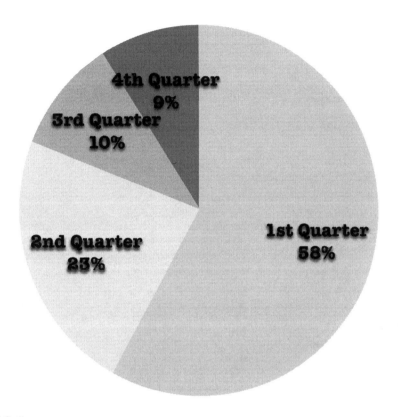

Example 14.1

What is the difference, to the nearest cent, between profits earned in quarter 3 and profits earned in quarter 4?

Solution:

$600.30

There is a one percentage point difference between profit earned in the 3rd quarter and profits earned in the 4th quarter. One percent of $60,030 is $600.30 (.01 • 60,030).

Alternatively, you could have calculated 10% of 60,030 and 9% of 60,030 and taken the difference.

Example 14.2

By approximately what percent did first quarter sales exceed that of second quarter sales?

Solution:

152%

To find the percent that 58 exceeds 23, use the percent change formula, given the base of 23:

$$\frac{(100)(58\%-23\%)}{23\%} = \frac{100(35\%)}{23\%} = \frac{100(.35)}{.23} = \frac{35}{.23} \approx 152\%$$

Note that you cannot simply subtract 23% from 58% to get 35%. That is a difference in percentage points, but not in percent.

Bar Graphs:

In bar graphs, data appears in rectangular blocks, the height or length of which are proportional to the values they represent.

.

Example 14.3

According to the graph below, where the x axis measures the number of tables sold and the y axis measures the revenue, approximately what percent would a customer save per table by purchasing 3 tables instead of 1?

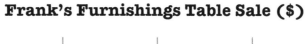

Frank's Furnishings Table Sale ($)

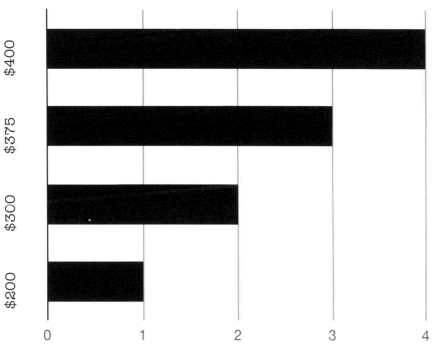

■ Number of Tables Purchased

Solution:

37.5%

One table costs $200. Purchasing three tables costs $375, or $125 each.

Thus, a customer saves $75 per table when purchasing three versus purchasing one, which is a savings of 75/200= 3/8= 37.5%.

Scatterplots:

Each point on a scatterplot corresponds to an ordered pair with data from the x axis and y axis respectively. Data shown on a scatterplot allow us to make inferences about the relationship or correlation between two variables. (For example, as x gets larger, does y seems to get larger or smaller?) Sometimes a scatterplot will reveal that there is no correlation between the variables.

In the scatterplot below, the highest point is (16, 125,000), meaning that someone in the data set has 16 years of education and is earning $125,000 per year.

Reference the scatterplot below for Examples **14.4 and 14.5:**

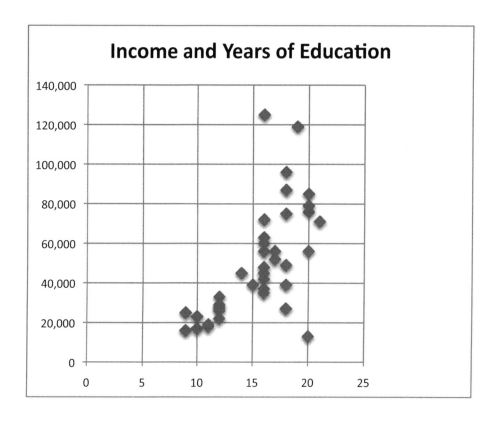

Example 14.4

Approximately how much could a high school dropout (fewer than 12 years of education) expect to earn, if his experience was in line with the trend of data above?

a) $15,000
b) $20,000
c) $30,000
d) $45,000
e) $55,000

Solution:

b

The values of those with education levels between 9 and 11 years are clustered around the $20,000 mark.

Example 14.5

One more person is to be added to the data pool. She has 18 years of education. How much could she earn?

Indicate all the answer choices that apply.

a) $12,000
b) $60,000
c) $180,000

Solution:

a, b, c

The additional person could earn any of the above (or any other value, for that matter). Scatterplots are a reflection of the given data and help identify that data trend. But that does not mean that any given data point will necessarily follow that trend.

Line Graphs:

Line graphs are good for showing trends over a period of time or when comparing how changes in inputs affect outputs.

Reference the graph below for Examples **14.6, 14.7, and 14.8**.

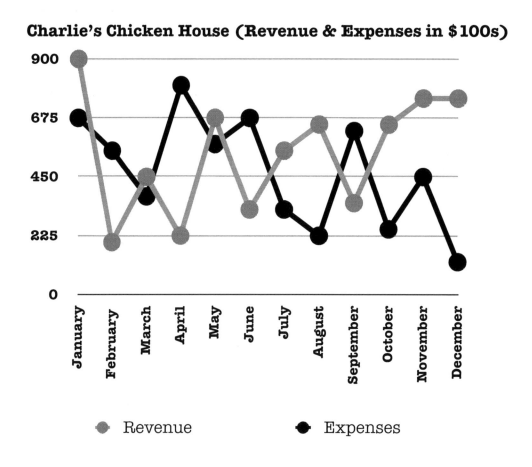

Charlie's Chicken House (Revenue & Expenses in $100s)

Example 14.6

Charlie's Chicken House made the greatest profit during which three-month period?

a) January to March
b) February to April
c) May to July
d) September to November
e) October to December

Solution:

e

To determine the answer to this question, this graph can be eye-balled: Only in the three-month period from October to December does revenue greatly exceed expense in each month.

In order to get exact values, you can add the revenues from the given three-month period and subtract the sum of the expenses over that period.

Example 14.7

For how many months did Charlie's Chicken House post a net profit?

a) 3
b) 4
c) 5
d) 7
e) 8

Solution:

e

In eight different months, the grey line (revenue) is above the black line (expense).

Example 14.8

What was the ratio of profits to expenses in November at Charlie's Chicken House?

Solution:

2:3

Charlie's Chicken House brought in $75,000 in revenue in November and had $45,000 in expenses. Thus, it's profit was $30,000 for the month of November. The profit to expense ratio is $30,000 : $45,000, or 2:3.

Frequency Tables:

Frequency tables are a way of representing data that have repeated values. Instead of listing each of the repeated values, the table has one column for the value and an adjacent column for its frequency.

The table below shows the number of siblings that each student in a sociology class has.

Example 14.9

Number of Siblings	Frequency
0	6
1	9
2	12
3	13
4	6
5	2
6	1
7	1

a) What is the mode of the data?

b) What is the median number of siblings in the group?

Solution:

a) **3**

The mode of the data is 3, because 13 students (which is the largest group of students) have 3 siblings each.

b) **2**

The median is between the 25th and 26th values, both of which fall under the category of 2 siblings.

Example 14.10

Number of Siblings	Relative Frequency
0	12%
1	18%
2	26%
3	24%
4	12%
5	4%
6	2%
7	2%

What percent of students have more than four siblings?

Solution:

8%

Eight percent (8%) of the students have 5 (4%), 6 (2%), or 7 (2%) siblings.

Example 14.11

Number of Siblings	Cumulative Frequency
0	12%
1	30%
2	56%
3	80%
4	92%
5	96%
6	98%
7	100%

What percent of people have 2 or 3 siblings?

Solution:

50%

From 1 sibling to 2 siblings, the cumulative frequency increases by 26% (56%-30%), and from 2 siblings to 3 siblings 24% (80% -56%). Thus, the total percent of people who have either 2 or 3 siblings is 50.

Venn Diagrams:

Visually, Venn Diagrams are comprised of two or more overlapping circles, where each circle represents a different category. The parts of the circles that overlap indicate those items which belong to two or more categories.

Consider the following example.

Example 14.12

Diamond's Car Dealership Lot

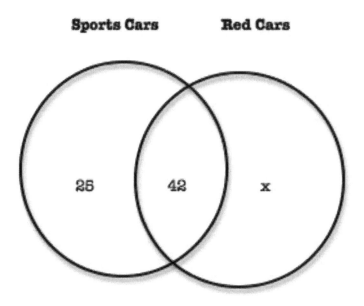

Sports Cars   Red Cars

25   42   x

1)

a) How many sports cars were on the Diamond's Dealership lot?

b) In terms of x, what is the ratio of the number of red cars to the number of non-red sports cars?

c) If there were twice as many red sports cars as there were red cars that were not sports cars, how many total cars were there that were sports cars, red cars, or both?

Solution:

a) **67**

Add the numbers that fall within the sports car circle.

b) **42 + x : 25**

The total number of red cars is 42 + x and the total number of non-red sports cars is 25.

c) **88**

There are 42 red sports cars, so there are 21 additional red cars that are not sports cars. That makes for a total of 88 cars that are red, sports cars, or both: 42 + 21 + 25.

CHAPTER 14 PRACTICE SET:

Reference the line graphs below for questions 1 and 2:

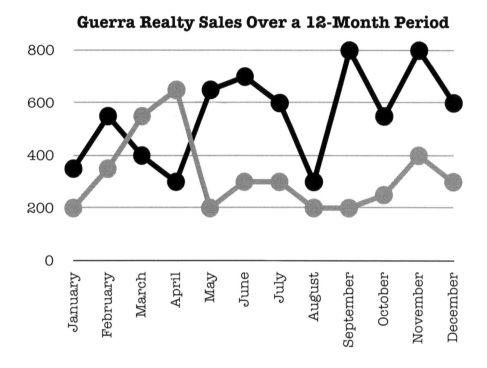

Guerra Realty Sales Over a 12-Month Period

● Number of Houses Sold/Month
● Average Housing Cost/Month (in $1,000s)

1) In what month were sales revenues lowest?

a) April

b) May

c) June

d) July

e) August

2) In what month did lower home costs seem to spur housing sales?

a) April

b) May

c) June

d) July

e) August

Reference the bar graph below for questions 3 and 4:

Number of Employees (in 1,000s) by Metro Area, 1999

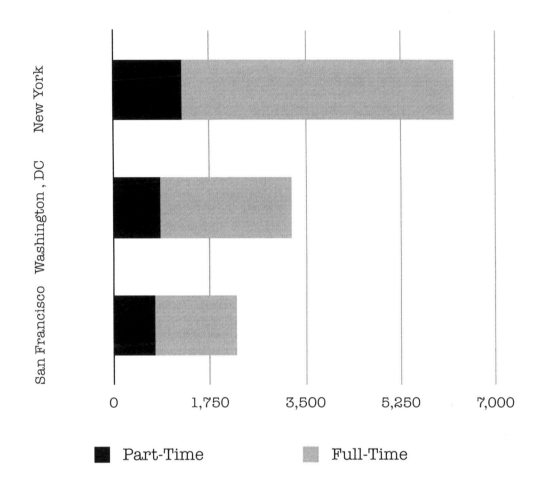

3) Which of the following has the greatest ratio?

a) Part-time to full-time in New York

b) Part-time to full-time in San Francisco

c) Full-time to part-time in Washington, DC

d) Part-time to all employees in San Francisco

e) All employees to part-time employees in New York

4) What percent of all jobs in the Washington, DC metro area were full-time in 1999?

a) 25

b) 33

c) 50

d) 75

e) 80

5)

The table below shows the number of siblings that each student in a sociology class has.

Number of Siblings	Frequency
0	6
1	9
2	12
3	13
4	6
5	2
6	1
7	1

Consider the table above. Among the sociology students who have 3 or fewer siblings, how many total siblings do they have between them?

a) 2

b) 6

c) 34

d) 40

e) 72

SOLUTIONS: Chapter 14 Practice Set

1) e
2) a
3) e
4) d
5) e

EXPLANATIONS: Chapter 14 Practice Set

1) **e**

Sales revenue was lowest in August, at $60,000,000. To calculate the revenue, multiply the number of homes sold that month (200) by the average housing cost for that month ($300,000).

Note that in this case there is actually no need to complete the operation or to find the dollar amount, as both the number of homes sold and the average cost of homes sold were lowest in August.

2) **a**

In April, housing costs were at their lowest and home sales were at their highest.

3) **e**

Note that in answer choices a, b, and d, the ratios are all less than one. Since the ratios are greater than one in both c and e, those are the only answer choices for which you need to estimate ratios.

Choice c: 2400:800 or 3:1

Choice e: 6,250: 1,250 or 5:1

4) **d**

There appears to have been roughly 3,200,000 jobs in 1999, 800,000 of which were part-time.

Full-time, therefore, is the difference: 3,200,000 - 800,000 = 2,400,000

$$\frac{2,400,000}{3,200,000} = \frac{3}{4} = 75\%$$

Therefore, full-time to all jobs is 2,400/3,200= .75= 75%

5) **e**

9 students have 1 sibling each: $9 \bullet 1 = 9$ siblings
12 students have 2 siblings each: $12 \bullet 2 = 24$ siblings
13 students have 3 siblings each: $13 \bullet 3 = 39$ siblings

Total siblings: 9 + 24 + 39 = 72.

Chapter 15: Strategies 101

Student: "These math explanations make perfect sense when you show me how to solve them—but on my own I wouldn't even know how to start some of the problems."

The above statement captures what many of my students have told me over the years. They get it when they see it explained, but they can't be expected to be exposed to every potential question. So then what?

There are several strategies and ways of thinking that can help you get through tough problems.

This chapter focuses on general strategies as well as ways to approach problems when you are stumped. Part of what makes you a strong GRE taker is remaining calm and working to piece together that which you do know in order to approach challenging questions.

Also, keep in mind that you are going to be very well prepared for the test. So, if you are intimately familiar with most types of questions, and you are able to answer such questions relatively quickly, you will have more time to reason out challenging questions.

General Strategies:

1) **Use Your Reasoning Skills.** Often we are so focused on recalling rules, principles, and formulas, or so engrossed in the details of a problem, that we lose perspective on what the problem is asking.

Example: After running the carnival, Joe divided the $22,000 profit between himself and his three partners. If the pay was distributed relative to the effort of each partner, what could have been the largest share, given that everyone earned a different amount?

Indicate all that apply.

a) 5,500
b) 11,000
c) 16,500
d) 19,000

Thought Process: If the money is divided evenly in a four-way split, each partner would get $5,500. However, since there is a largest share, that share must be more than $5,500. (If you're not convinced, play around with different breakdowns—at least one share is always greater than $5,500.) Therefore, choices b, c, and d are all possible.

---

2) **Turn the Abstract into the Concrete.** Imagine you bought p pencils, discounted d percent, from an original price of c cents each. How much did you end up paying?... Say what?... This problem is doable through direct solving. However, when you are given a problem with several unknowns, note that the relationship between the unknowns holds no matter what the problem is. Therefore, you can a) choose values for each variable, b) answer the question based on these values, and c) plug your values into the answer choices to see which one yields the same value.

Example: Inez bought p pencils discounted d percent from an original price of c cents each. How much did she end up paying (in dollars)?

a) $.01 \bullet (100 - d)\% \bullet c \bullet p$
b) $.01 \bullet d\% \bullet c \bullet p$
c) $100 \bullet d \bullet c \bullet p$
d) $100d\% \bullet c \bullet p$
e) $100 \bullet (100 - d)\% \bullet c \bullet p$

Thought Process: Let p = 10, d = 25, and c = 100. That means that Inez bought 10 pencils, originally for $1 each (100 cents) at a 25% discount (which is 25 cents off). Then, answer the question: Therefore, Inez paid 75 cents each for 10 pencils, for a total of $7.50.

Next, go through each answer choice, plugging in p=10, d=25, and c= 100, looking to see which one gives you $7.50 as an answer. (Note, however, that if more than one answer choice gives you $7.50, you will have to choose a different set of numbers and go through the process again, this time testing only the remaining choices.)

The correct answer is a.

Example : If bc = 35 a, and $\dfrac{c}{a}$ = 10, what is the value of b?

Thought Process: In order to figure out the value of b using the first equation, we must have values for a and c. However, a and c can be any values, as long as the quotient of c and a is 10. Therefore, choose numbers for c and a, like c= 20 and a=2. Then, plug the result into the first equation:

$bc = 35a$

$b \cdot 20 = 35 \cdot 2$ Substitute 2 and 20 in for a and c, respectively

$20b \;\; = 70$ Simplify

$b \;\; = \dfrac{70}{20}$ Divide both sides by 20

$b \;\; = \dfrac{7}{2}$ Reduce

3) **When you get stuck, write down everything you know.** That is, write down everything you know that seems to relate to the problem. Sometimes it is not obvious how to solve a problem, even when you are familiar with the concept and understand the question. But once you get started, the path to solving the problem becomes apparent.

Example: The average of x, y, and z is 36. What is the average of x and y?

a) $12 - \dfrac{z}{3}$

b) $18 + \dfrac{z}{4}$

c) $36 - \dfrac{z}{3}$

d) $54 - \dfrac{z}{2}$

e) $108 + \dfrac{z}{3}$

Thought Process: We are being asked to find the average of x and y. Finding the average requires us to know the sum of x and y. If we can find the sum of x, y, and z, we can subtract the value of z to get the sum of x and y.

How do we get the sum of x, y, and z? The average formula is the sum divided by the number of numbers.

Therefore, the sum = average • 3 = 36 • 3 = 108.

Since x + y + z = 108, x+y = 108 - z. Therefore, the average of x and y is:

$$\frac{x+y}{2} = \frac{108-z}{2}$$

$$\frac{x+y}{2} = 54 - \frac{z}{2}$$

The correct answer is d.

Example: If the circumference of a circle is 32π, what is its area?

Thought Process: The question itself is straightforward: What is the area of the circle? However, at first consideration, the process to solve it might not be. So start with what you are being asked, and work backwards: In order to find the area, you need to use the formula $A = \pi r^2$. But you don't know what r, the radius is. Hmmm. Well, you're told that the circumference is 32π, so how can that help? Start by writing down the circumference formula: $C = 2\pi r$, and then setting the value equal to the given circumference: $32\pi = 2\pi r$. By solving for the radius (by dividing both sides by 2π), you see that r= 16. You can now input the value of r into the area formula to get 256π.

4) **Test the Middle Answer Choice First.** In questions that have numbers in the answer choice, note that the answer choices are arranged in ascending order. If you are going to test the answer choices to see which one is the solution, start with the middle choice. That way, if you find that your choice is too large, you can eliminate the choices that are even larger, and whittle down the potential answer choices to the two smaller answers. Or, if you find your answer choice is too small, you can eliminate the ones that are even smaller.

Example: From 2011 to 2012, discounted movie tickets at Save 'n View Theaters went up in price by 30% to $6.50. What was the entry fee in 2011?

a) $4.55
b) $5.00
c) $5.50
d) $5.75
e) $6.15

Thought Process: The answer choices represent the potential entry fee of the movie theater in 2011. Let's first see if the answer is C. Find 30% of $5.50. That's $1.65. The total price, then, would be $7.15. Since this is too high, the answer must be less than $5.50.

Test either answer choice a or b. If the one you test is right, that's the answer. If you one you test is wrong, the other answer choice is the answer. Since $5.00 is an easier number to work with, find 30% of $5.00. That's $1.50. Add the $1.50 on to the $5.00 and you find that the 2012 ticket price is $6.50.

Note that if you had simply taken 30% off of $6.50 (the 2012 price), you would have ended up with answer choice a. This is the wrong approach because the 30% change is based off of the original ticket price, not the new ticket price.

The correct answer is b.

5) **Make 100 your friend.** When dealing with abstract questions that involve percents, base your number off of 100. This makes it easy to find various percents of your original number. For example, 30% of 100 is 30 and 127% of 100 is 127.

Example: The City of Dale decreased in population by 20% from 1990 to 1991, and then increased by 5% the following year. The population at the end of 1992 was what percent of the original population?

a) 75
b) 84
c) 88
d) 92
e) 95

Thought Process: Imagine that the original population was 100. A 20% decrease would have left the population at 80. The following year the population increased by 5% of its current population of 80. This is a net gain of 4 in the population, for a total population of 84.

The population at the end of 1992, then, is b, 84% of the 1990 population.

---

6) **Be sure to answer the question.** There's nothing worse than working out all the math correctly and then answering the wrong question—for example, determining the value of x when you are asked for, say, the value of x + 8. The test writers know the common mistakes that test takers make. So, if you do most of the steps correctly and then fail to answer the

question being asked, more than likely the answer you come up with will be an answer choice—but a wrong one.

Also, the more questions you practice, the more likely you'll be to encounter a similar question. But remember, many questions have a twist or a slight variation. Make sure you are answering the question you are being asked, as opposed to answering the question you think you are being asked. Read carefully!

Example: Kai spent $150 of her savings on her new purchases. If that represents 30% of her original savings, how much money does she have left?

Thought Process: $150 represents 30% of her savings. A percent proportion allows you to figure out how much money she had saved:

$$\frac{150}{x} = \frac{30}{100}$$

$$15,000 = 30x$$

$$\frac{15,000}{30} = \frac{30x}{30}$$

$$500 = x$$

So, Kai originally had $500 in savings. Now, let's be sure to answer the question. How much money does she have left?: $500-$150 = $350.

7) **For Quantitative Comparison questions, whenever possible, do a comparison rather than a calculation.** Often it saves time to compare the two given columns, manipulating them so that they look as similar as possible—as opposed to evaluating the columns. It differs by question, but make it a goal to work as efficiently as possible. So, when comparing over calculating is possible, comparing should always win out.

Example:

Quantity A	Quantity B
$9(12 + 10 + 8 + 6 + 4 + 2)$	$10(9 + 7 + 5 + 3 + 1)$

Thought Process: If we were to distribute, each of the first five terms in Column A would be greater than each of the corresponding five terms in Column B. Therefore, Column A is greater.

8) **For multiple choice questions with more than one answer, sometimes you can find the lowest and highest answer, and include all the values in between.** In other words, depending on the context of the question, you might be able to find the lower bound and upper bound of the answer, and include the answer choice with in-between values.

Example:

David's birthday is on February 29th, which only comes around on leap year (once every four years). If David has had only 11 birthdays, how many years old could he be?

Indicate <u>all</u> answer choices that apply.

a) 42
b) 43
c) 44
d) 45
e) 46
f) 47
g) 48

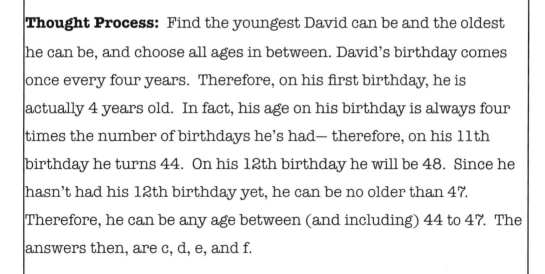

Thought Process: Find the youngest David can be and the oldest he can be, and choose all ages in between. David's birthday comes once every four years. Therefore, on his first birthday, he is actually 4 years old. In fact, his age on his birthday is always four times the number of birthdays he's had— therefore, on his 11th birthday he turns 44. On his 12th birthday he will be 48. Since he hasn't had his 12th birthday yet, he can be no older than 47. Therefore, he can be any age between (and including) 44 to 47. The answers then, are c, d, e, and f.

9) **Remember that the GRE is not the end all be all.** While it is very important to go into the test having prepared your best, know that having to take the test a second time is not the end of the world. If something goes horribly wrong, you have an opportunity to cancel your scores before they are submitted. Or, if upon finding out your scores you realize they are lower than you need, you can always take the test again. Of course you don't want to take the test again, but reminding yourself that this is not your one and only shot can take some pressure off of you, allowing you to think clearly and do your best the first time around.

Example: Karen spent m% of her salary buying $\sqrt{k}$% of her wardrobe, leaving her overdrawn by \$p in her checking account, because she forgot she had spent h% of her salary on the rent. What percent of her wardrobe should she return in order to pull her account out of the negatives?

Thought Process: What the?!?!?!?!?! Is this question serious? I'm going for a beer! (Now, that's the spirit!)

296

About the Author

A self-proclaimed teacher by the age of six, Julia Andrews found her first students among her stuffed animal collection. Upon getting her first crack at living, breathing students at the age of 15, she was hooked. She's been tutoring students for the GRE specifically since 2003 after earning a near perfect score on the exam herself.

Along the way Ms. Andrews has earned degrees in math, economics, and public policy, and taught math in a Washington, DC middle school and for various test prep and tutoring firms. She now runs Andrews Tutoring in Takoma Park, MD, where she has the privilege of working with wonderful students, from elementary-aged children to mid-career professionals looking to return to school.

When she isn't tutoring students or thinking about tutoring students, Ms. Andrews often can be found spending time with her family, eating delicious food, or running off the delicious food she ate.

She'd love to hear from you: julia@andrewstutoring.com.